Prepared in cooperation with the Kansas Water Office

Suspended-Sediment Loads, Reservoir Sediment Trap Efficiency, and Upstream and Downstream Channel Stability for Kanopolis and Tuttle Creek Lakes, Kansas, 2008–10

Scientific Investigations Report 2011–5187

U.S. Department of the Interior
U.S. Geological Survey

Suspended-Sediment Loads, Reservoir Sediment Trap Efficiency, and Upstream and Downstream Channel Stability for Kanopolis and Tuttle Creek Lakes, Kansas, 2008–10

By Kyle E. Juracek

Prepared in cooperation with the Kansas Water Office

Scientific Investigations Report 2011–5187

U.S. Department of the Interior
U.S. Geological Survey

U.S. Department of the Interior
KEN SALAZAR, Secretary

U.S. Geological Survey
Marcia K. McNutt, Director

U.S. Geological Survey, Reston, Virginia: 2011

For more information on the USGS—the Federal source for science about the Earth, its natural and living resources, natural hazards, and the environment, visit http://www.usgs.gov or call 1–888–ASK–USGS.

For an overview of USGS information products, including maps, imagery, and publications,
visit http://www.usgs.gov/pubprod

To order this and other USGS information products, visit http://store.usgs.gov

Suggested citation:
Juracek, K.E., 2011, Suspended-sediment loads, reservoir sediment trap efficiency, and upstream and downstream channel stability for Kanopolis and Tuttle Creek Lakes, Kansas, 2008–10: U.S. Geological Survey Scientific Investigations Report 2011–5187, 35 p.

ISBN 978-1-4113-3278-2

Acknowledgments

This study was made possible, in part, by support from the Kansas Water Office and the Kansas State Water Plan Fund. The author gratefully acknowledges Chris Gnau (Kansas Water Office) for providing a technical review of the report.

Several U.S. Geological Survey individuals also are recognized for their invaluable assistance in the completion of this study. For operation and maintenance of water-quality monitors, completion of water-quality records, and collection of suspended-sediment samples, the author gratefully acknowledges the following individuals: Trudy Bennett, Andrew Clark, Craig Dare, Patrick Finnegan, Jackline Gatotho, Slade Hackney, Dirk Hargadine, Bill Holladay, Eric Looper, Lori Marintzer, Deneise Schneider, Travis See, Mandy Stone, and Nathan Sullivan. For assistance with database development, the author gratefully acknowledges Brian Klager. Finally, for providing a technical review of the report, the author gratefully acknowledges David Heimann and David Mau.

Contents

Figures

Tables

Conversion Factors

Inch/Pound to SI

Multiply	By	To obtain
Length		
inch (in.)	2.54	centimeter (cm)
inch (in.)	25.4	millimeter (mm)
foot (ft)	0.3048	meter (m)
mile (mi)	1.609	kilometer (km)
Area		
square mile (mi^2)	259.0	hectare (ha)
square mile (mi^2)	2.590	square kilometer (km^2)
Volume		
cubic foot (ft^3)	0.02832	cubic meter (m^3)
cubic foot (ft^3)	0.00002296	acre-foot (acre-ft)
acre-foot (acre-ft)	1,233	cubic meter (m^3)
Flow rate		
cubic foot per second (ft^3/s)	0.02832	cubic meter per second (m^3/s)
Mass		
pound (lb)	0.4536	kilogram (kg)
ton	2,000	pound (lb)
ton	0.9072	megagram (Mg)
ton per day (ton/d)	0.9072	metric ton per day
ton per year (ton/yr)	0.9072	metric ton per year

Suspended-Sediment Loads, Reservoir Sediment Trap Efficiency, and Upstream and Downstream Channel Stability for Kanopolis and Tuttle Creek Lakes, Kansas, 2008–10

By Kyle E. Juracek

Abstract

Continuous streamflow and turbidity data collected from October 1, 2008, to September 30, 2010, at streamgage sites upstream and downstream from Kanopolis and Tuttle Creek Lakes, Kansas, were used to compute the total suspended-sediment load delivered to and released from each reservoir as well as the sediment trap efficiency for each reservoir. Ongoing sedimentation is decreasing the ability of the reservoirs to serve several purposes including flood control, water supply, and recreation. River channel stability upstream and downstream from the reservoirs was assessed using historical streamgage information.

For Kanopolis Lake, the total 2-year inflow suspended-sediment load was computed to be 600 million pounds. Most of the suspended-sediment load was delivered during short-term, high-discharge periods. The total 2-year outflow suspended-sediment load was computed to be 31 million pounds. Sediment trap efficiency for the reservoir was estimated to be 95 percent. The mean annual suspended-sediment yield from the upstream basin was estimated to be 129,000 pounds per square mile per year. No pronounced changes in channel width were evident at five streamgage sites located upstream from the reservoir. At the Ellsworth streamgage site, located upstream from the reservoir, long-term channel-bed aggradation was followed by a period of stability. Current (2010) conditions at five streamgages located upstream from the reservoir were typified by channel-bed stability. At the Langley streamgage site, located immediately downstream from the reservoir, the channel bed degraded 6.15 feet from 1948 to 2010.

For Tuttle Creek Lake, the total 2-year inflow suspended-sediment load was computed to be 13.3 billion pounds. Most of the suspended-sediment load was delivered during short-term, high-discharge periods. The total 2-year outflow suspended-sediment load was computed to be 327 million pounds. Sediment trap efficiency for the reservoir was estimated to be 98 percent. The mean annual suspended-sediment yield from the upstream basin was estimated to be 691,000 pounds per square mile per year. In general, no pronounced changes in channel width were evident at six streamgage sites located upstream from the reservoir. At the Barnes and Marysville streamgage sites, located upstream from the reservoir, long-term channel-bed degradation followed by stability was indicated. At the Frankfort streamgage site, located upstream from the reservoir, channel-bed aggradation of 1.65 feet from 1969 to 1989 followed by channel-bed degradation of 2.4 feet from 1989 to 2010 was indicated and may represent the passage of a sediment pulse caused by historical disturbances (for example, channelization) in the upstream basin. With the exception of the Frankfort streamgage site, current (2010) conditions at four streamgages located upstream from the reservoir were typified by channel-bed stability. At the Manhattan streamgage site, located downstream from the reservoir, high-flow releases associated with the 1993 flood widened the channel about 60 feet (30 percent). The channel bed at this site degraded 4.2 feet from 1960 to 1998 and since has been relatively stable.

For the purpose of computing suspended-sediment concentration and load, the use of turbidity data in a regression model can provide more reliable and reproducible estimates than a regression model that uses discharge as the sole independent variable. Moreover, the use of discharge only to compute suspended-sediment concentration and load may result in overprediction.

Stream channel banks, compared to channel beds, likely are a more important source of sediment to Kanopolis and Tuttle Creek Lakes from the upstream basins. Other sediment sources include surface-soil erosion in the basins and shoreline erosion in the reservoirs.

Introduction

In Kansas and nationally, sedimentation is a concern as it progressively reduces the capacity of reservoirs to serve various purposes including flood control, water supply, and recreation. Kanopolis Lake is a Federal impoundment on the Smoky Hill River in Ellsworth County, central Kansas (fig. 1). Officially completed by the U.S. Army Corps of Engineers (USACE) in 1948, Kanopolis Lake has lost an estimated 34 percent of its water-storage capacity in the conservation (multi-purpose) pool to sedimentation as of 2010 (Kansas Water Office, 2010a) at a rate of about 0.5 percent annually. Tuttle Creek Lake is a Federal impoundment on the Big Blue River in Pottawatomie and Riley Counties, northeast Kansas (fig. 2). Officially completed by USACE in 1962, Tuttle Creek Lake has lost an estimated 43 percent of its water-storage capacity in the conservation (multi-purpose) pool to sedimentation as of 2010 (Kansas Water Office, 2010b) at a rate of about 0.9 percent annually.

Concern about the condition of Tuttle Creek Lake was evidenced by the listing of the reservoir under Section 303(d) of the Federal Clean Water Act of 1972 for sedimentation (Kansas Department of Health and Environment, 2010). The 303(d) list is a priority list that identifies water bodies that do not meet water-quality standards that are based on the use of the water bodies. For each impaired water body on the 303(d) list, a State is required by the Federal Clean Water Act to develop a total maximum daily load (TMDL), which is an estimate of the maximum pollutant load (material transported during a specified time period) from point and nonpoint sources that a receiving water can accept without exceeding water-quality standards (U. S. Environmental Protection Agency, 1991). Kanopolis Lake was not on the 303(d) list for sedimentation as of 2010.

The development of sediment management plans to extend the projected life of both reservoirs requires an understanding of the amount of sediment delivered to each reservoir, the amount of sediment retained in each reservoir, and river channel stability. To provide some of the required information, a 3-year study by the U.S. Geological Survey (USGS), in cooperation with the Kansas Water Office, was begun in 2008. Specific objectives of the study were to:

1. Compute the suspended-sediment loads delivered to and released from Kanopolis and Tuttle Creek Lakes;

2. Estimate the suspended-sediment trap efficiency for Kanopolis and Tuttle Creek Lakes; and

3. Assess the stability of river channels upstream and downstream from Kanopolis and Tuttle Creek Lakes.

Purpose and Scope

The purpose of this report is to present the results of the USGS study to compute suspended-sediment loads delivered to and released from Kanopolis and Tuttle Creek Lakes, and to estimate the suspended-sediment trap efficiency of both reservoirs from October 1, 2008, to September 30, 2010. Also presented are the results of an assessment of channel stability upstream and downstream from both reservoirs. Study objectives were met by the collection of continuous streamflow and turbidity data at inflow and outflow sites for both reservoirs, the collection of discrete water samples at the inflow and outflow sites that were analyzed for suspended-sediment concentration, and the analysis of historical USGS streamgage information. Results presented in this report will assist the Kansas Water Office in efforts to evaluate sediment management options for the reservoirs and upstream basins. From a national perspective, the methods and results presented in this report will provide guidance and perspective for future reservoir studies concerned with sediment management issues.

Description of Kanopolis and Tuttle Creek Lake Basins

The Kanopolis Lake Basin is an area of 7,857 mi^2 (square miles) that drains part of central and west-central Kansas as well as part of east-central Colorado (fig. 1). Physiographically, the basin is located in the High Plains and Plains Border sections of the Great Plains Province (Fenneman, 1946). The High Plains section in the upstream one-third of the basin is typified by flat plains with limited stream dissection and little local relief. This section is underlain by fluvial (stream) and eolian (windblown) sediment deposits that consist of clay, silt, sand, and gravel. The Plains Border section in the downstream two-thirds of the basin is more dissected than the High Plains section and, thus, has greater local relief. This section is underlain by limestone, shale, and sandstone, with minor fluvial and eolian deposits. Long-term mean annual precipitation in the basin ranges from about 19 in. (inches) at Sharon Springs, Kansas (period of record 1893–2009), in the western part of the basin (fig. 1), to about 28 in. at Ellsworth, Kansas (period of record 1904–2009), in the eastern part (fig. 1) (High Plains Regional Climate Center, 2010). Most of the annual precipitation is received during the growing season (generally April-September). Land use (2005) in the basin is mostly agricultural with cropland and grassland accounting for about 53 and 46 percent of the basin, respectively. Urban land use and woodland each occupy less than 1 percent of the basin (Kansas Applied Remote Sensing Program, 2009).

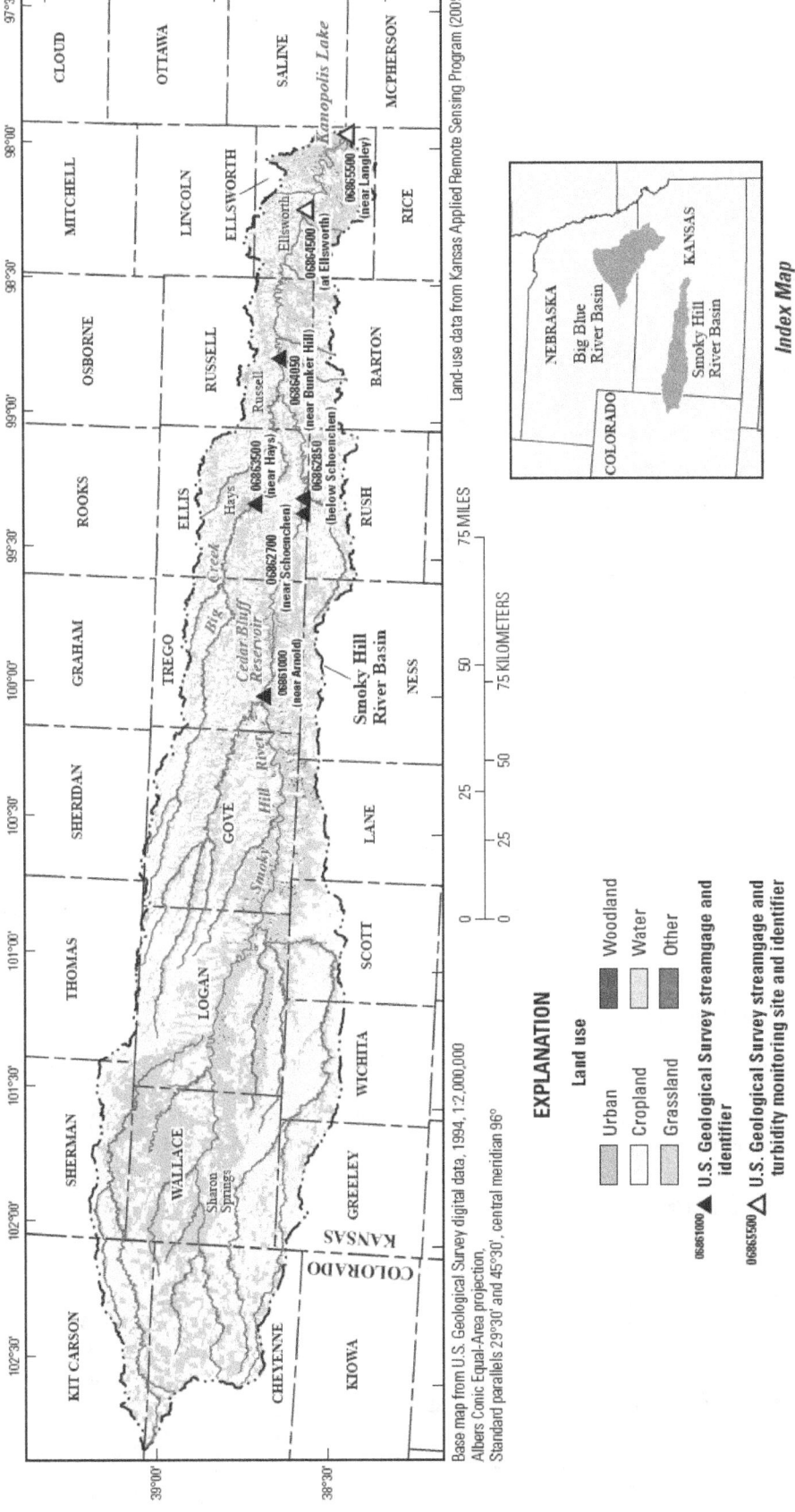

Base map from U.S. Geological Survey digital data, 1994, 1:2,000,000
Albers Conic Equal-Area projection,
Standard parallels 29°30' and 45°30', central meridian 96°

Land-use data from Kansas Applied Remote Sensing Program (2009)

EXPLANATION

Land use

- Urban
- Cropland
- Grassland
- Woodland
- Water
- Other

▲ U.S. Geological Survey streamgage and identifier
06861000

△ U.S. Geological Survey streamgage and turbidity monitoring site and identifier
06865500

Index Map

Figure 1. Kanopolis Lake Basin, Kanopolis Lake, selected U.S. Geological Survey streamgages, and land use (2005) in the Kanopolis Lake Basin, east-central Colorado and west-central Kansas.

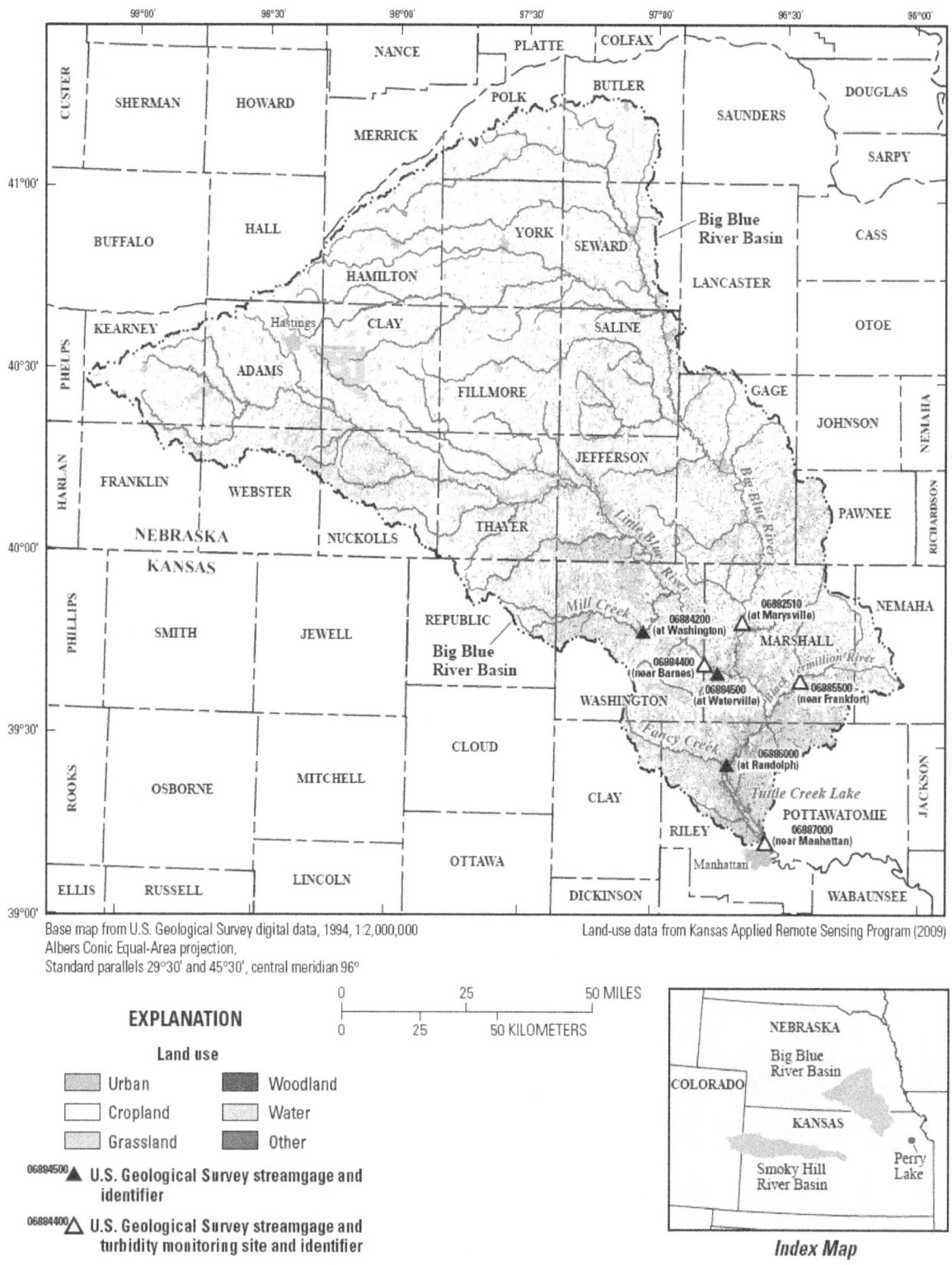

Figure 2.   Tuttle Creek Lake Basin, Tuttle Creek Lake, selected U.S. Geological Survey streamgages, and land use (2005) in the Tuttle Creek Lake Basin, southeast Nebraska and northeast Kansas.

The Tuttle Creek Lake Basin, which essentially is synonymous with the Big Blue River Basin (except for the small area located downstream from the dam) is an area of 9,628 mi^2 that drains parts of southeast Nebraska and northeast Kansas (fig. 2). About 75 percent of the basin is located in Nebraska. Physiographically, the upstream one-half of the basin is located mostly in the High Plains and Plains Border sections of the Great Plains Province (Fenneman, 1946) (similar to the Kanopolis Lake Basin). The downstream one-half of the basin is located mostly in the Dissected Till Plains section of the Central Lowland Province (Fenneman, 1946). This section is characterized by dissected deposits of glacial till that consist of clay, silt, sand, gravel, and boulders that overlie bedrock of primarily shale and limestone, with some sandstone (Jordan and Stamer, 1995). Long-term mean annual precipitation in the basin ranges from about 26 in. at Hastings, Nebraska (period of record 1894-2009), in the northwest part of the basin (fig. 2), to about 33 in. at Manhattan, Kansas (period of record 1893–2009), in the southeast (High Plains Regional Climate Center, 2010). Most of the annual precipitation is received during the growing season (generally April–September). Land use (2005) in the basin is mostly agricultural with cropland and grassland accounting for about 70 and 24 percent of the basin, respectively. Woodland accounts for about 4 percent of the basin. Urban land use occupies about 1 percent of the basin (Kansas Applied Remote Sensing Program, 2009).

Methods

The objectives of the study were accomplished using newly collected and historical information. For the purposes of estimating suspended-sediment loads and reservoir sediment trap efficiency, continuous streamflow and turbidity data and suspended-sediment samples were collected at USGS streamgage sites located upstream and downstream from Kanopolis and Tuttle Creek Lakes. Turbidity has been shown to be a frequently reliable predictor of suspended-sediment concentration (Rasmussen and others, 2009). For the purpose of assessing channel stability upstream and downstream from the reservoirs, historical USGS streamgage information for multiple sites was used.

Continuous Streamflow and Water-Quality Monitoring

Continuous streamflow data for the inflows to, and outflows from, Kanopolis and Tuttle Creek Lakes were collected as part of the USGS national streamgaging network using standard USGS methods (Turnipseed and Sauer, 2010). For this study, streamflow data for October 1, 2008, through September 30, 2009, (water year 2009) and October 1, 2009, through September 30, 2010, (water year 2010) were used. For Kanopolis Lake, inflow data were collected at the Smoky Hill River at Ellsworth (hereafter Ellsworth) streamgage

(station 06864500, fig. 1, table 1). The Ellsworth streamgage monitors the inflow from about 96 percent of the basin upstream from the reservoir. Outflow data for Kanopolis Lake were collected at the Smoky Hill River near Langley (hereafter Langley) streamgage (station 06865500, fig. 1, table 1).

Inflow data for Tuttle Creek Lake were collected at the Big Blue River at Marysville (hereafter Marysville) streamgage (station 06882510), the Little Blue River near Barnes (hereafter Barnes) streamgage (station 06884400), and the Black Vermillion River near Frankfort (hereafter Frankfort) streamgage (station 06885500) (fig. 2, table 1). Together, these three streamgages monitor the inflow from about 89 percent of the basin upstream from the reservoir. Outflow data for Tuttle Creek Lake were collected at the Big Blue River near Manhattan (hereafter Manhattan) streamgage (station 06887000, fig. 2, table 1).

Continuous hourly turbidity data were collected during the 2009 and 2010 water years at the Barnes, Ellsworth, Frankfort, Manhattan, and Marysville streamgage sites. For this purpose, a YSI monitor (model 6600 or 600 OMS) with an optical turbidity sensor (model 6136) was used. The YSI 6136 turbidity sensor can measure turbidity over a published range of 0 to 1,000 formazin nephelometric units (FNUs) (YSI, 2007). At all five sites, the YSI monitor was housed in an open-ended polyvinyl chloride (PVC) pipe drilled with holes to allow stream water to flow through the installation. At Barnes, Ellsworth, Frankfort, and Manhattan, the monitor was suspended from a bridge by chain in the main flow zone of the river. At Marysville, the monitor was attached to the side of an abandoned structure next to an overflow dam located about one-half mile upstream from the streamgage site. Turbidity data for Langley were collected periodically using a handheld YSI monitor lowered from a bridge. The objective for Langley was to collect turbidity data that were representative of the range of releases from Kanopolis Lake.

Because in-stream turbidity conditions occasionally may exceed the upper measurement limit of the YSI 6136 turbidity sensor, optical-backscatter Hach SOLITAX sc turbidity and suspended-solids sensors (SOLITAX) also were installed at Barnes, Ellsworth, Frankfort, and Marysville. The SOLITAX sensor can measure suspended-solids concentration over a published range of 0 to 50,000 milligrams per liter (mg/L) (Hach Company, 2005). At each site, the SOLITAX sensor was housed in an open-ended PVC pipe and installed in the same manner as the YSI monitor. YSI 6136 turbidity data and SOLITAX suspended-solids data are strongly correlated over a range of conditions (fig. 3).

The YSI 6136 turbidity time-series data occasionally were truncated because in-stream turbidity conditions exceeded the upper measurement limit for the sensors. In addition, YSI turbidity time-series data sometimes were missing or deleted from the continuous record because of equipment malfunctions or sensor fouling. To provide a complete hourly turbidity data set, data for these periods were estimated. For periods of stable streamflow, hourly turbidity values were estimated by interpolation (Rasmussen and Ziegler, 2003;

Table 1.   U.S. Geological Survey streamgages used in this study.

[All streamgages listed were used for channel-stability analyses. Streamgages listed in **bold** also were used for turbidity monitoring and suspended-sediment sample collection. USGS, U.S. Geological Survey; mi², square miles]

USGS streamgage number (figs. 1 and 2)	USGS streamgage name	Drainage area (mi²)	Period of record
	Kanopolis Lake		
06862700	Smoky Hill River near Schoenchen, KS	5,750	1964–2010
06862850	Smoky Hill River below Schoenchen, KS	5,810	1981–2010
06863500	Big Creek near Hays, KS	549	1947–2010
06864050	Smoky Hill River near Bunker Hill, KS	7,075	1939–2010
06864500	**Smoky Hill River at Ellsworth, KS**	**7,580**	**1928–2010**
06865500	**Smoky Hill River near Langley, KS**	**7,857**	**1940–2010**
	Tuttle Creek Lake		
06882510	**Big Blue River at Marysville, KS**	**4,777**	**1984–2010**
06884200	Mill Creek at Washington, KS	344	1959–2010
06884400	**Little Blue River near Barnes, KS**	**3,351**	**1958–2010**
06884500	Little Blue River at Waterville, KS	3,509	1928–1958
06885500	**Black Vermillion River near Frankfort, KS**	**410**	**1953–2010**
06886000	Big Blue River at Randolph, KS	9,100	1918–1960
06887000	**Big Blue River near Manhattan, KS**	**9,640**	**1953–2010**

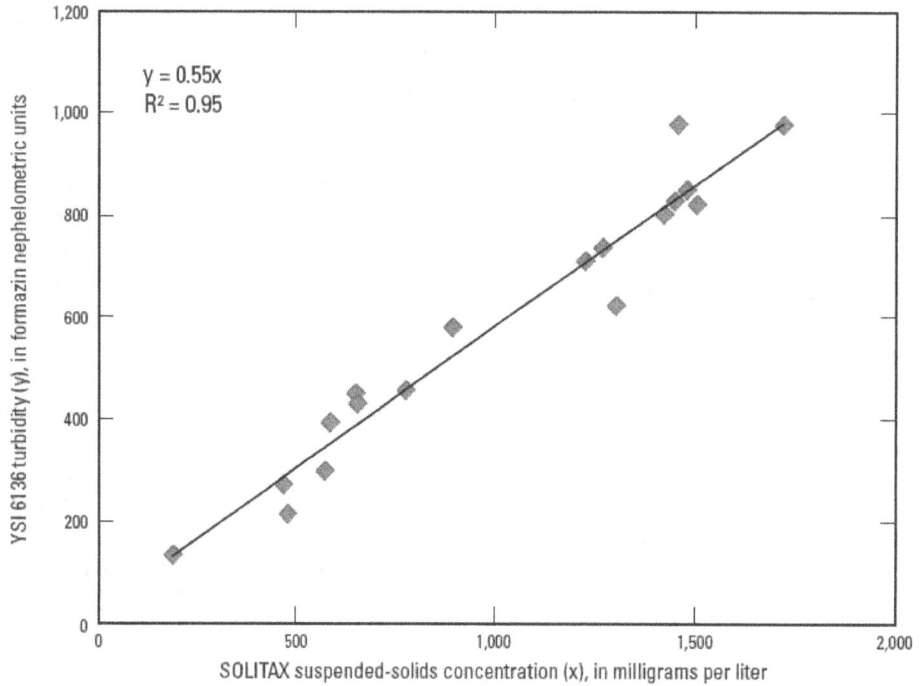

Figure 3.   Relation between YSI 6136 turbidity data and SOLITAX suspended-solids concentration data at streamgage sites upstream from Kanopolis and Tuttle Creek Lakes, 2010. R^2 is the coefficient of determination.

Rasmussen and others, 2005). For periods of changing stream-flow, hourly turbidity data were estimated using SOLITAX data, if available. In these cases, turbidity was estimated using a YSI-to-SOLITAX ratio. If SOLITAX data were unavailable, hourly turbidity data for periods of changing streamflow were estimated by interpolation.

At each site, the sensors were cleaned and calibrated approximately every 2 months. Additional cleaning visits were made when real-time data indicated errors caused by environmental fouling. Quality-assurance checks were made before and after sensor cleaning and calibration using an independently calibrated sensor. Sensor cleaning and calibration were done in accordance with guidance provided by Wagner and others (2006).

Suspended-Sediment Sample Collection and Analysis

Suspended-sediment samples were collected at all inflow and outflow monitoring sites for Kanopolis and Tuttle Creek Lakes (figs. 1 and 2) using equal-width increment (EWI) methods as described in Nolan and others (2005). At each inflow site, a total of 14–15 samples were collected that provide data for a range of streamflow and turbidity conditions. At each outflow site, a total of 9–10 samples were collected that provide data for a range of reservoir releases. All samples were analyzed for suspended-sediment concentration (SSC). Selected samples also were analyzed for particle-size distribution [percent of suspended sediment (by weight) less than 100, 63, 31, 16, 8, 4, and 2 μm (micrometers) in diameter]. All SSC and particle-size analyses were performed at the USGS Sediment Laboratory in Iowa City, Iowa, using methods described by Guy (1969). For each EWI sample, turbidity was measured for a single vertical sample (collected from the main flow zone during the collection of the EWI sample) using a Hach 2100AN turbidimeter (Hach Company, 2000). Analysis of suspended-sediment samples for turbidity using the Hach 2100AN turbidimeter were performed at the USGS laboratory in Lawrence, Kansas.

Quality Assurance

Quality assurance was provided by evaluations of variability for turbidity measurements and SSC analyses. During the collection of suspended-sediment samples, turbidity was measured across the width of the stream. Median turbidity values of the cross-sectional measurements were compared with the in-stream (fixed location) sensor at each site to assess the ability of the in-stream sensor to provide turbidity data that were representative across the width of the stream. As part of each comparison, the coefficient of determination (R^2) was

computed. The R^2 is the fraction of the variance explained by a regression model (Helsel and Hirsch, 1992). It provides an indication of the goodness of fit of a model (that is, its ability to accurately model a data set). The larger the R^2 (up to a maximum possible value of 1.0), the more reliable is the model. The comparisons indicated that the in-stream sensors generally provided turbidity data that were representative of conditions across the width of each stream as evidenced by the R^2 that was 0.91 or larger for each site (fig. 4).

To assess variability in the SSC analyses, duplicate suspended-sediment samples were collected and analyzed for SSC. With one exception, SSC values for the duplicate samples were within 10 percent of the original samples. The exception was a duplicate sample collected at the Manhattan streamgage site for which the SSC value was 20 percent smaller (table 2).

Regression Models

Ordinary-least-squares regression analysis was used to develop statistical relations between in-stream turbidity and SSC, between in-stream turbidity, discharge and SSC, and between discharge and suspended-sediment load (SSL). The regression models, used for the purpose of computing hourly SSC and SSL, were developed in accordance with procedures described by Rasmussen and others (2009). All data were log-transformed in order to better approximate normality and to even the variability in regression residuals. After development and application of the regression models, SSC and SSL values were retransformed back to linear space. Because retransformation can introduce bias, a bias correction factor (Duan's smearing estimator; Duan, 1983) was used as a multiplier to correct the retransformed SSC and SSL values (Helsel and Hirsch, 1992).

Development of the regression models to compute SSC using in-stream turbidity (and sometimes also discharge) required that each suspended-sediment sample had an associated turbidity value. For samples collected during periods when the in-stream YSI 6136 turbidity was less than or equal to 1,000 FNU, the average YSI 6136 turbidity during the time of sample collection was used. For samples collected during periods when the in-stream YSI 6136 turbidity was truncated (that is, larger than 1,000 FNU) or otherwise unavailable, the YSI 6136 turbidity was computed based on the turbidity measured for a single vertical sample (collected from the main flow zone during the collection of the EWI sample) using a Hach 2100AN turbidimeter (Hach Company, 2000). YSI 6136 turbidity data and Hach 2100AN turbidity data are strongly correlated (fig. 5). A simple regression model, unique for each monitoring site, was used to estimate in-stream YSI 6136 turbidity using Hach 2100AN turbidity data.

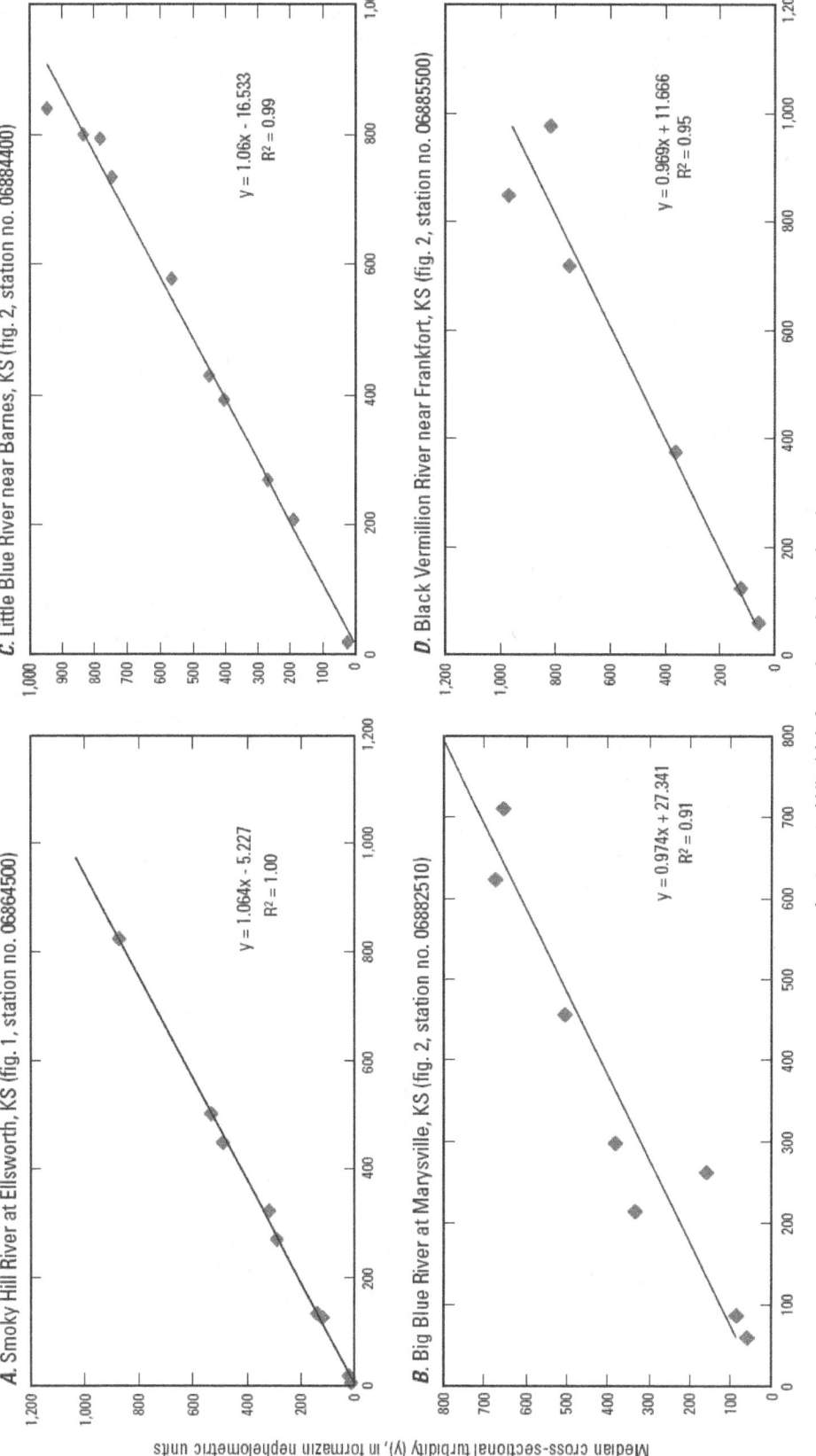

Figure 4.   Relation between cross-sectional median and in-stream (fixed location) turbidity measurements for streamgage sites upstream from Kanopolis and Tuttle Creek Lakes, 2008–10. R² is the coefficient of determination.

Table 2. Suspended-sediment concentrations for original and duplicate suspended-sediment samples collected at Kanopolis and Tuttle Creek Lake streamgage sites, 2008–10.

[Results for duplicate samples are listed parenthetically. ft³/s, cubic feet per second; FNU, formazin nephelometric units; mg/L, milligrams per liter; >, greater than; --, not available]

Date of sample collection (month/day/year)	Discharge (ft³/s)	Turbidity[1] (FNU)	Suspended-sediment concentration (mg/L)	Percentage difference between duplicate and original sample
Smoky Hill River at Ellsworth, KS (fig. 1, station no. 06864500)				
03/05/10	70	19	40 (40)	0
06/11/10	350	503	747 (759)	1.6
Big Blue River at Marysville, KS (fig. 2, station no. 06882510)				
10/30/09	1,500	262	275 (260)	-5.5
Little Blue River near Barnes, KS (fig. 2, station no. 06884400)				
03/10/10	2,920	800	2,940 (2,670)	-9.2
04/30/10	3,730	>1,000	5,370 (5,560)	3.5
Black Vermillion River near Frankfort, KS (fig. 2, station no. 06885500)				
03/25/10	2,730	848	2,530 (2,610)	3.2
05/21/10	1,080	374	1,090 (1,030)	-5.5
Big Blue River near Manhattan, KS (fig. 2, station no. 06887000)				
10/07/08	1,580	--	45 (36)	-20

[1]Turbidity measured by in-stream (fixed location) YSI model 6136 turbidity sensor.

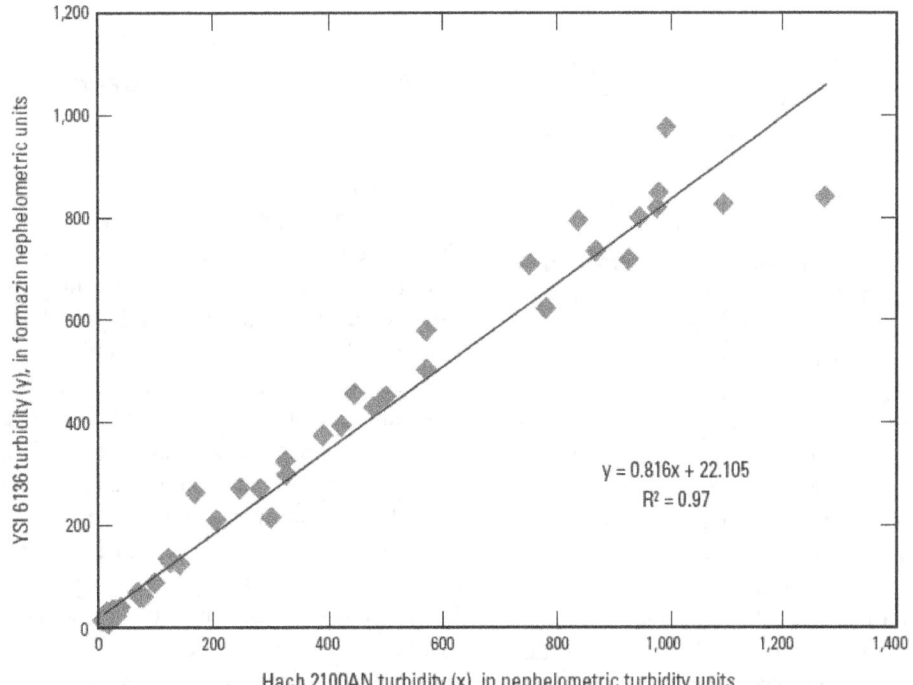

$$y = 0.816x + 22.105$$
$$R^2 = 0.97$$

Figure 5. Relation between in-stream YSI 6136 turbidity data and laboratory Hach 2100AN turbidity data for Kanopolis and Tuttle Creek Lake streamgage sites, 2008–10. R^2 is the coefficient of determination.

Computation of Sediment Concentrations, Loads, and Yields

Instantaneous SSC was computed for each hour of the 2-year period of record using regression models developed for the relation between in-stream YSI 6136 turbidity (and sometimes also discharge) and SSC for the Barnes, Ellsworth, Frankfort, Manhattan, and Marysville streamgage sites. The resultant log-transformed SSC values were retransformed back to linear space and corrected for potential retransformation bias by multiplying by a bias correction factor (Duan, 1983). Instantaneous SSL was calculated using the following equation:

$$SSL_i = SSC_i \times Q_i \times c, \qquad (1)$$

where

SSL_i is the computed instantaneous suspended-sediment load, in pounds per second;

SSC_i is the computed instantaneous suspended-sediment concentration for the ith value, in milligrams per liter;

Q_i is the instantaneous discharge for the ith value, in ft³/s (cubic feet per second), and

c is a constant, 6.242×10^{-5} (Rasmussen and others, 2009).

Hourly SSL was computed for each hour of the 2-year period of record by multiplying the instantaneous SSL by 3,600.

For the Langley streamgage site, instantaneous SSL was computed for each hour of the 2-year period of record using a regression model developed for the relation between SSL and discharge. This approach was used because continuous turbidity data were not available for this site. The resultant log-transformed SSL values were retransformed back to linear space and corrected for potential retransformation bias by multiplying by a bias correction factor (Duan, 1983). As before, hourly SSL was computed for each hour of the 2-year period of record by multiplying the instantaneous SSL by 3,600.

The total SSL for each of the four inflow and two outflow streamgage sites was computed as the sum of the hourly SSL values for the 2-year period. The total inflow SSL for Kanopolis Lake was estimated as the total SSL computed for the Ellsworth streamgage multiplied by 1.04 to account for the 4 percent of the Kanopolis Lake Basin that was not monitored. The total inflow SSL for Tuttle Creek Lake was estimated as the sum of the total SSLs computed for the Barnes, Frankfort, and Marysville streamgages multiplied by 1.11 to account for the 11 percent of the Tuttle Creek Lake Basin that was not monitored. Use of the multiplier required the assumption that the SSL originating from the unmonitored part of each basin was similar to the SSL originating from the monitored part of each basin on a per unit area basis.

For Kanopolis Lake, the total inflow SSL was affected by the presence of Cedar Bluff Reservoir, which is located about 120 river mi (miles) upstream from the Ellsworth streamgage

(fig. 1). At the Smoky Hill River near Arnold streamgage (station 06861000, fig. 1), which is located about 23 river mi upstream from the dam at Cedar Bluff Reservoir, the mean annual discharge for 1951 to 2010 was 38 ft³/s. In comparison, the mean annual discharge for 1951 to 2010 at the Ellsworth streamgage was 239 ft³/s (U.S. Geological Survey, 2011). The adjusted mean annual discharge at Ellsworth in the absence of Cedar Bluff Reservoir was estimated to be about 277 ft³/s; that is, about 16 percent larger. Because there generally is a direct relation between discharge and SSL, it is reasonable to propose that, in the absence of Cedar Bluff Reservoir (and its storage of virtually all of the inflow discharge and SSL), there would be an increase in the total inflow SSL to Kanopolis Lake of similar magnitude.

Mean annual suspended-sediment yield for each reservoir basin was estimated as the total SSL for the 2-year period divided by two then divided by basin area. The basin area for Kanopolis Lake was computed by subtracting the basin area upstream from Cedar Bluff Reservoir (5,530 mi²) from the total basin area for Kanopolis Lake (7,857 mi²). This adjustment was made based on an assumption that no SSL was contributed by the outflow from Cedar Bluff Reservoir. The assumption was made because typically no releases are made from the reservoir (Bill Peck, Bureau of Reclamation, oral commun., 2011). Therefore, the basin area upstream from Cedar Bluff Reservoir typically was noncontributing. All of the SSL delivered to Kanopolis Lake was assumed to originate from the part of the basin located downstream from Cedar Bluff Reservoir.

Estimation of Reservoir Sediment Trap Efficiency

Reservoir sediment trap efficiency provides an indication of the proportion of the total inflow suspended-sediment load that is deposited and permanently stored within a reservoir. For this study, trap efficiency was estimated for Kanopolis and Tuttle Creek Lakes for the 2-year period that consisted of the 2009 and 2010 water years. Trap efficiency for both reservoirs was estimated as the total deposited suspended-sediment load (computed as total inflow suspended-sediment load minus total outflow suspended-sediment load) divided by the total inflow suspended-sediment load and expressed as a percentage. The total inflow and outflow suspended-sediment loads for Kanopolis Lake were estimated using data collected at the Ellsworth and Langley streamgages, respectively (fig. 1). For Tuttle Creek Lake, the total inflow suspended-sediment load was estimated using data collected at the Barnes, Frankfort, and Marysville streamgages (fig. 2). The total outflow suspended-sediment load for Tuttle Creek Lake was estimated using data collected at the Manhattan streamgage (fig. 2). Because the contribution of sediment from shoreline erosion was not accounted for, the estimated trap efficiencies may be conservative.

Channel-Stability Analysis

A geomorphic analysis of channel stability was completed for 13 USGS streamgages located upstream and downstream from Kanopolis and Tuttle Creek Lakes (figs. 1 and 2, table 1). Typically, streamgages provide the only long-term, continuous source of channel-geometry information for the sites being monitored. Streamgage information can be used for various geomorphic purposes including documentation of channel changes (for example, channel-bed erosion or deposition, or channel-width change), reconstruction of historical channel conditions, estimation of process rates, and the estimation of future channel changes (Juracek and Fitzpatrick, 2009). In this study, the geomorphic analysis was focused on an assessment of channel stability at each streamgage site as evidenced by changes in channel-bed elevation and channel width.

At any given location and time along a stream, a relation exists between stage (that is, the height of the water in the channel above a given datum) and discharge (that is, streamflow volume per unit time). For streamgages, these relations are quantified on rating curves and updated as necessary to accommodate changes in channel shape, slope, and other factors that affect the relations. Each rating curve represents a best-fit line through the measurement data (that is, paired measurements of stage and discharge). Discharge measurements at, and stage-discharge ratings for, USGS streamgages are made using standard USGS techniques (Kennedy, 1984; Turnipseed and Sauer, 2010) with a typical accuracy of about ±5 percent (Kennedy, 1983; Sauer and Meyer, 1992; Turnipseed and Sauer, 2010).

By computing the stage that relates to a reference discharge for each rating curve developed during the period of record of a streamgage (and correcting to a common datum, if necessary), trends in the elevation of the channel bed can be inferred by plotting the resulting time-series data. Ideally, the reference discharge selected is a relatively low flow that is sensitive to change. Use of a low discharge minimizes the effects of variations in channel width on flow depth (Simon and Hupp, 1992). Reference discharges previously used have included the mean annual discharge for the period of record (Juracek, 2004) and the discharge exceeded 95 percent of the time (Williams and Wolman, 1984). In this study, the mean annual discharge for the period of record was used as the reference discharge to investigate possible changes in channel-bed elevation.

A statistical test was used to determine the significance of any observed trends in channel-bed elevation change. For this purpose, a nonparametric Spearman's rho correlation coefficient was computed. An advantage of Spearman's rho is that, because it is based on ranks, it is more resistant to outlier effects than the more commonly used Pearson's r correlation coefficient (Helsel and Hirsch, 1992). Measures of correlation are dimensionless and scaled to be in the range of -1.0 to 1.0. A value of 0 indicates no relation between two variables. Temporal trends were considered to be significantly positive (with

a value between 0 and 1.0) or negative (with a value between 0 and -1.0) if the probability (two-sided p-value) of rejecting a correct hypothesis (in this case, no trend) was less than or equal to 0.05.

If the stage for the reference discharge (hereafter referred to as the reference stage) has a downward trend, it may be inferred that the channel-bed elevation has declined with time because of degradation (erosion). Conversely, if the reference stage has an upward trend, it may be inferred that the channel-bed elevation has risen with time as a result of aggradation (deposition). An abrupt increase or decrease in reference stage may be indicative of a relatively rapid change in channel-bed elevation. The absence of a pronounced change or trend indicates that the channel bed essentially has been stable.

Changes in channel width were assessed through an analysis of discharge-width relations. Here, width refers to water-surface width data available for individual discharge measurements. For each streamgage site, discharge-width relations were grouped into approximate 5-year successive intervals (to get a representative range of in-channel flow conditions) that covered the period of record. Plotting of the successive intervals was used to determine if channel width changed with time.

Several possible limitations may restrict or prevent the use of streamgage data to assess channel stability. First, for an area of interest, there may be an inadequate number of streamgages with a sufficiently long period of record. Second, an existing streamgage may not be ideal because it is located in a reach that is unrepresentative or essentially stable as a result of one or more natural or human-caused conditions. Third, discharge measurements made at different cross sections (locations) may be a concern because the potential variability introduced may affect interpretation of geomorphic change. For a comprehensive discussion of the potential limitations of using streamgage data for geomorphic applications see Juracek and Fitzpatrick (2009).

To supplement the streamgage information, 2005–08 aerial photography (U. S. Department of Agriculture, Farm Service Agency, 2010) and onsite inspections were used to examine the river channels for evidence of current and recent channel-bank erosion.

Characterization of Sediment Loading To and From Reservoirs

Hydrologic Conditions

To provide an indication of how reservoir inflows for water years 2009 and 2010 (that is, the 2-year study period) compared to historical conditions, the annual mean discharges for the period of record were examined for the upstream streamgage(s) for each reservoir. Because there generally is a direct relation between discharge and SSL, the variability in annual mean discharge also provides an indication of the year-to-year variability in SSL delivered to each reservoir. For Kanopolis Lake, the annual mean discharges for water years 2009 and 2010 at the Ellsworth streamgage (station 06864500, fig. 1, table 1) were similar (that is, within 20 percent) to the median annual discharge for the period of record (158 ft³/s) (U.S. Geological Survey, 2011) (fig. 6).

Inflows to Tuttle Creek Lake were monitored at three upstream streamgages—Barnes (station 06884400), Frankfort (station 06885500), and Marysville (station 06882510) (fig. 2, table 1). The annual mean discharge for the Barnes streamgage was 22 percent smaller than the median annual discharge for the period of record (631 ft³/s) for water year 2009 and 49 percent larger for water year 2010 (U.S. Geological Survey, 2011) (fig. 7A). Compared to the median annual discharge for the period of record (140 ft³/s), the annual mean discharge for the Frankfort streamgage was 15 percent larger for water year 2009 and 99 percent larger for water year 2010 (U.S. Geological Survey, 2011) (fig. 7B). The annual mean discharge for the Marysville streamgage was 18 percent smaller than the median annual discharge for the period of record (886 ft³/s) for water year 2009 and 45 percent larger for water year 2010 (U.S. Geological Survey, 2011) (fig. 7C).

Streamflow duration curves were created to enable a comparison of the distribution of streamflow values at and among the streamgages located upstream from the reservoirs for the 2009 and 2010 water years. Specifically, the duration curves show the frequency of exceedance of streamflow values for each site. For Kanopolis Lake, the duration curve for the Ellsworth streamgage is provided in figure 8. For Tuttle Creek Lake, the duration curves for the Barnes, Frankfort, and Marysville streamgages are provided in figure 9.

Regression Models

Regression models were developed for the purpose of computing hourly SSC and SSL for the 2-year study period at each streamgage (table 3, fig. 10). Each regression model was developed using a model calibration data set that consisted of discrete samples for which SSC, turbidity, and discharge were determined (table 4).

In addition to SSC, the particle-size distribution (seven size classes) of the suspended sediment was determined for most of the samples collected at the streamgages located upstream from Kanopolis and Tuttle Creek Lakes. The median percentage of silt and clay (particles less than 63 μm in diameter) for samples collected at the Ellsworth, Barnes, Frankfort, and Marysville streamgage sites was 96, 89, 94, and 96 percent, respectively (table 4). Particle-size analyses for samples collected at the streamgages located downstream from the two reservoirs were limited to a determination of the percentage of silt and clay because of the small amount of suspended sediment in the samples. The median percentage of silt and clay for samples collected at the Langley and Manhattan streamgage sites was 86 and 92 percent, respectively (table 4).

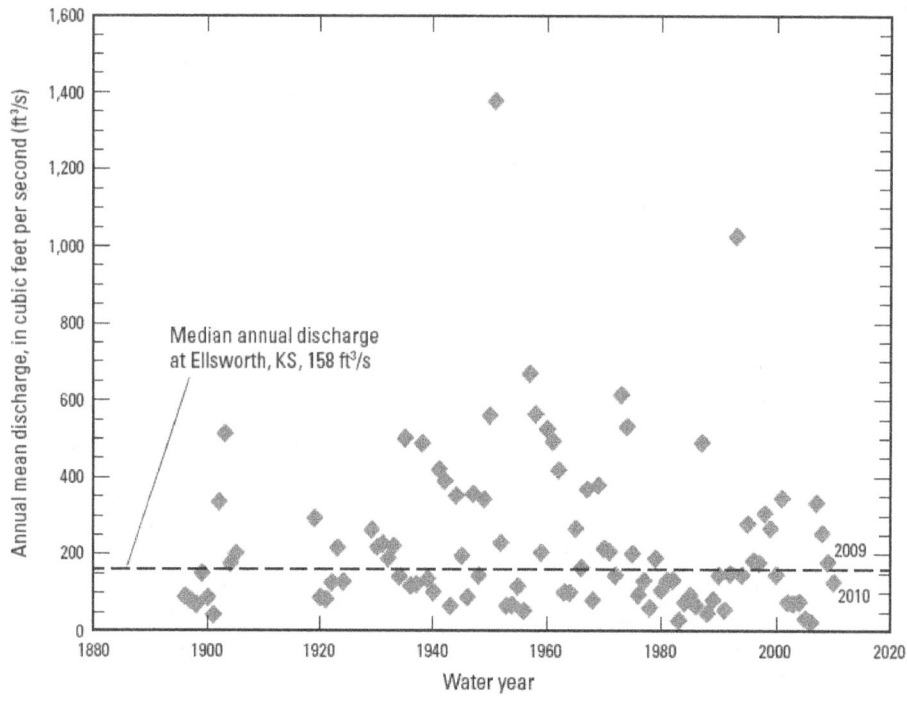

Figure 6.   Variation in annual mean discharge at Smoky Hill River at Ellsworth streamgage (station 06864500), 1896–2010.

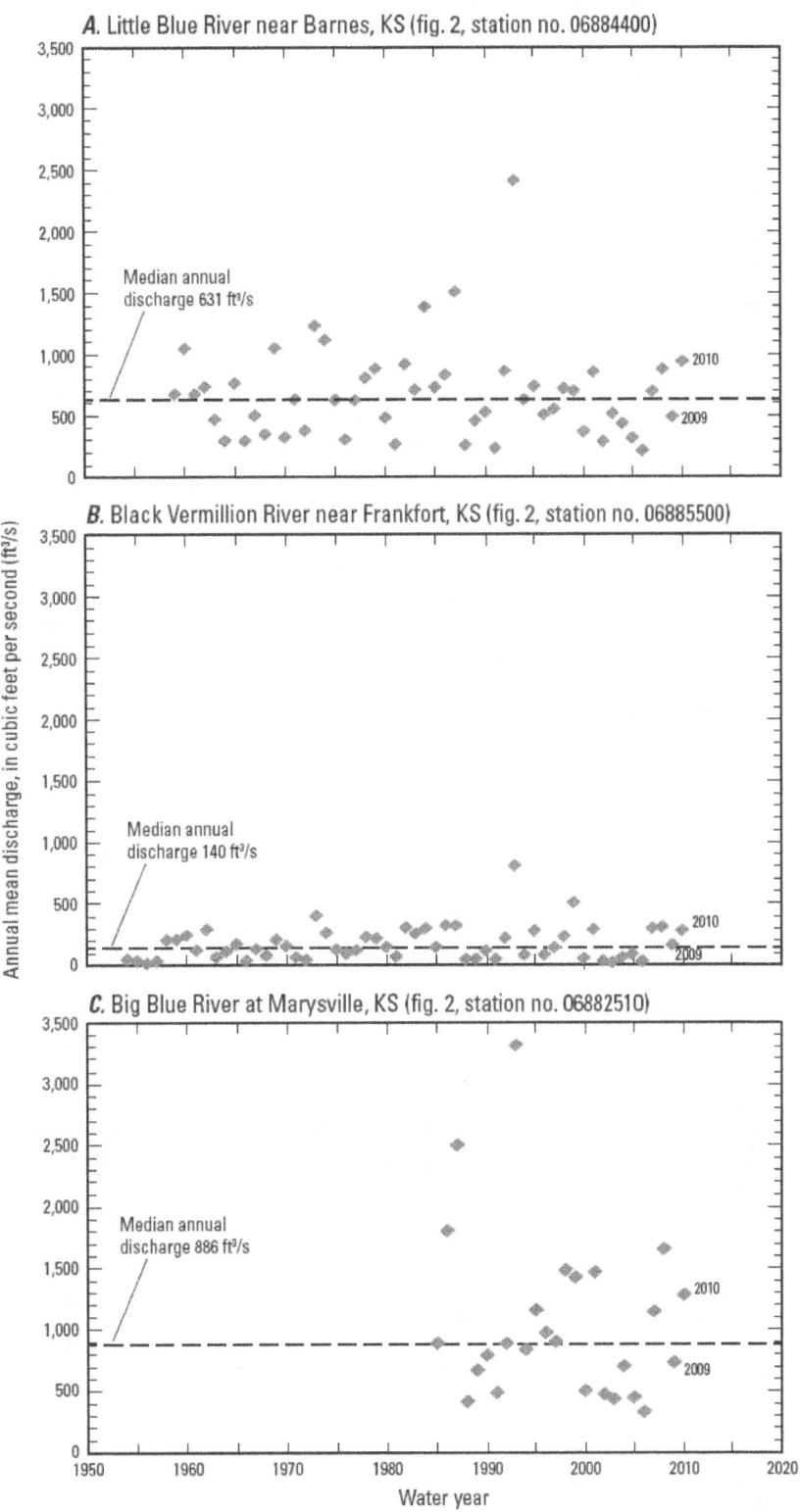

Figure 7. Variation in annual mean discharge at (*A*) Little Blue River near Barnes streamgage (station 06884400), 1959–2010; (*B*) Black Vermillion River near Frankfort streamgage (station 06885500), 1954–2010; and (*C*) Big Blue River at Marysville streamgage (station 06882510), 1985–2010.

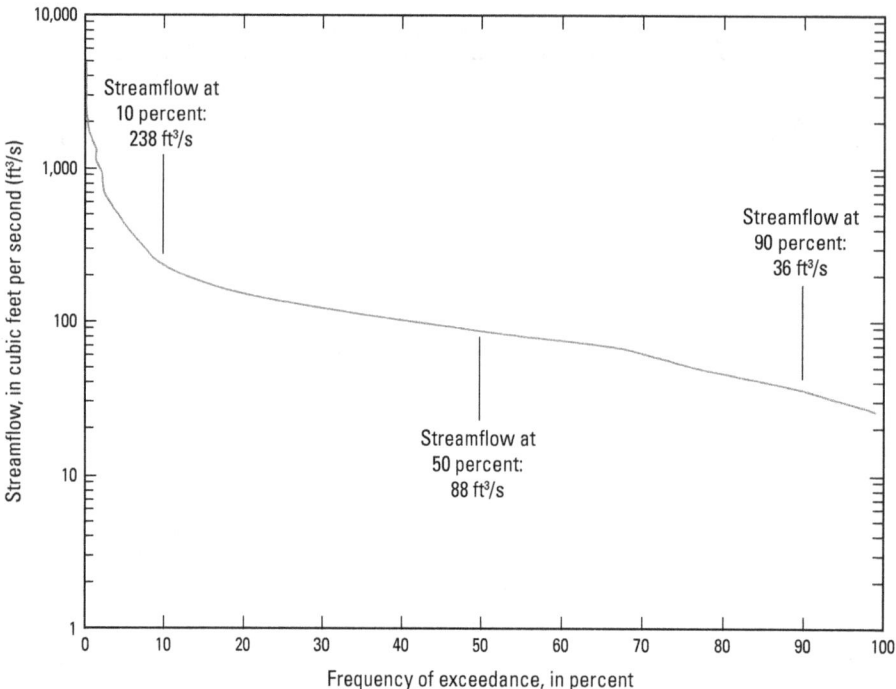

Figure 8.   Streamflow duration curve for the Smoky Hill River at Ellsworth streamgage (station 06864500), water years 2009 and 2010.

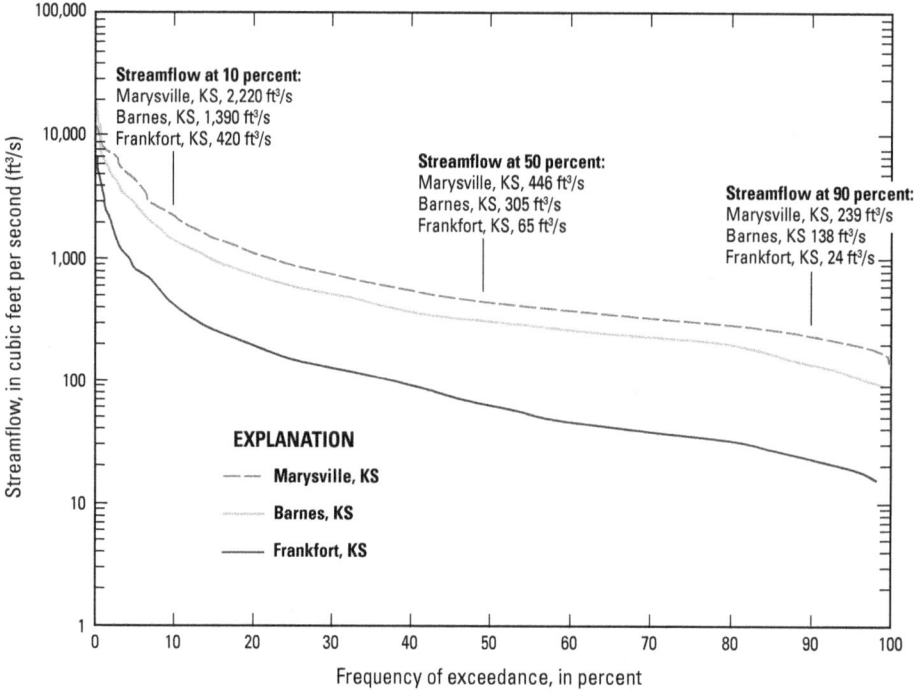

Figure 9.   Streamflow duration curves for the Little Blue River near Barnes (station 06884400), the Black Vermillion River near Frankfort (station 06885500), and the Big Blue River at Marysville (station 06882510) streamgages, water years 2009 and 2010.

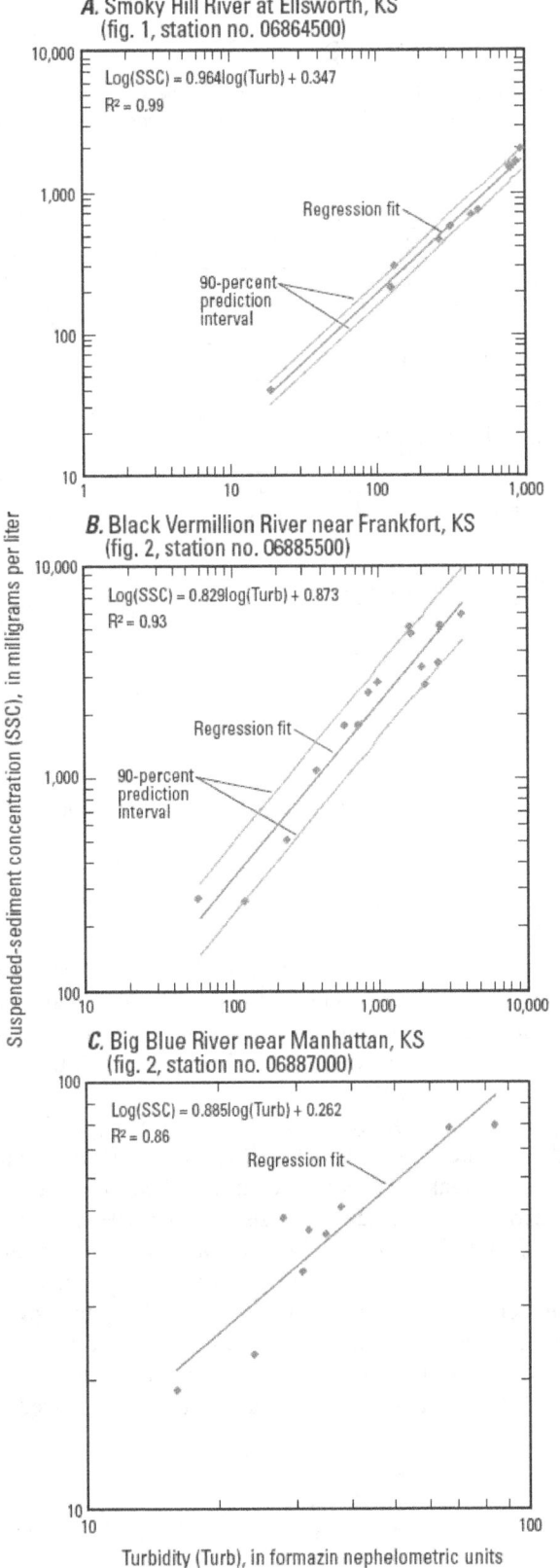

A. Smoky Hill River at Ellsworth, KS
(fig. 1, station no. 06864500)

Log(SSC) = 0.964log(Turb) + 0.347
R² = 0.99

Regression fit

90-percent
prediction
interval

B. Black Vermillion River near Frankfort, KS
(fig. 2, station no. 06885500)

Log(SSC) = 0.829log(Turb) + 0.873
R² = 0.93

Regression fit

90-percent
prediction
interval

C. Big Blue River near Manhattan, KS
(fig. 2, station no. 06887000)

Log(SSC) = 0.885log(Turb) + 0.262
R² = 0.86

Regression fit

Suspended-sediment concentration (SSC), in milligrams per liter

Turbidity (Turb), in formazin nephelometric units

Figure 10. Regression models used to compute suspended-sediment concentration based on turbidity at (*A*) the Smoky Hill River at Ellsworth (station 06864500), (*B*) the Black Vermillion River near Frankfort (station 06885500), and (*C*) the Big Blue River near Manhattan (station 06887000) streamgages, water years 2009 and 2010. R² is the coefficient of determination.

Sediment Loads, Yields, and Reservoir Sediment Trap Efficiencies

Total inflow SSL for Kanopolis and Tuttle Creek Lakes was computed for the monitored part of each basin and adjusted to account for the unmonitored part of each basin. The total 2-year inflow SSL to Kanopolis Lake was computed to be 600 million lb (pounds). Mean annual suspended-sediment yield for the Kanopolis Lake Basin was estimated to be 129,000 lb/mi²/yr (pounds per square mile per year). The total 2-year outflow SSL from Kanopolis Lake was computed to be 31 million lb. Sediment trap efficiency for Kanopolis Lake was estimated to be 95 percent (fig. 11).

The relation between discharge and SSL in the inflow to Kanopolis Lake was demonstrated by a comparison of total discharge to total SSL for water years 2009 and 2010 at the Ellsworth streamgage site (fig. 1). In water year 2009, total discharge was 5.67 billion ft³ (cubic feet) and total SSL was 406 million lb. In water year 2010, total discharge was 4.05 billion ft³ (29 percent less) and total SSL was 171 million lb (58 percent less). For the 2-year monitoring period at the Ellsworth streamgage, the standardized SSL, computed as the total SSL divided by the total discharge, was 0.06 lb/ft³ (pound per cubic foot of water) or 1.29 tons/acre-ft (tons per acre-foot).

For Tuttle Creek Lake, the total 2-year inflow SSL was computed to be 13.3 billion lb. Contributions to the total SSL estimated for the Barnes, Marysville, and Frankfort streamgage sites were 41, 38, and 11 percent, respectively. The remaining 10 percent of the total SSL was attributed to the unmonitored part of the basin. Mean annual suspended-sediment yield for the Tuttle Creek Lake Basin was estimated to be 691,000 lb/mi²/yr. The total 2-year outflow SSL from Tuttle Creek Lake was computed to be 327 million lb. Sediment trap efficiency for Tuttle Creek Lake was estimated to be 98 percent (fig. 12).

The relation between discharge and SSL in the inflow to Tuttle Creek Lake was demonstrated by a comparison of total discharge to total SSL for water years 2009 and 2010 at the Barnes, Marysville, and Frankfort streamgage sites (fig. 2). At Barnes, total discharge and total SSL for water year 2009 were 15.5 billion ft³ and 1.60 billion lb, respectively. In water year 2010, total discharge was 29.7 billion ft³ (92 percent larger) and total SSL was 3.87 billion lb (142 percent larger). At Marysville, total discharge and total SSL for water year 2009 were 23.0 billion ft³ and 1.37 billion lb, respectively. In water year 2010, total discharge was 40.4 billion ft³ (76 percent larger) and total SSL was 3.75 billion lb (174 percent larger). At Frankfort, total discharge and total SSL for water year 2009 were 5.08 billion ft³ and 574 million lb, respectively. In water year 2010, total discharge was 8.80 billion ft³ (73 percent larger) and total SSL was 825 million lb (44 percent larger).

Standardized SSL for the 2-year monitoring period, computed as previously described, was compared for the three streamgage sites located upstream from Tuttle Creek Lake. Respectively, the standardized SSLs for

Table 3. Regression models used for computing suspended-sediment concentrations and loads.

[R^2, coefficient of determination; MSPE, model standard percentage error; FNU, formazin nephelometric units; SSC, suspended-sediment concentration; mg/L, milligrams per liter; Turb, turbidity in formazin nephelometric units; %, percent; Q, discharge in cubic feet per second; SSL, suspended-sediment load]

Regression model	Duan bias correction[1]	R^2	Mean MSPE[2]	Number of samples	Range in turbidity[3] (FNU)	Range in SSC (mg/L)
Smoky Hill River at Ellsworth, KS (fig. 1, station no. 06864500)						
Log(SSC) = 0.964log(Turb) + 0.347	1.007	0.99	13%	11	19–975	40–2,020
Smoky Hill River near Langley, KS (fig. 1, station no. 06865500)						
Log(SSL) = 1.369log(Q) – 3.564	1.13	0.89	61%	9	14–34	14–100
Big Blue River at Marysville, KS (fig. 2, station no. 06882510)						
Log(SSC) = 0.543log(Turb) + 0.63log(Q) – 0.612	1.02	0.97	24%	14	59–3,006	107–4,870
Little Blue River near Barnes, KS (fig. 2, station no. 06884400)						
Log(SSC) = 0.731log(Turb) + 0.312log(Q) + 0.148	1.02	0.97	22%	15	21–3,148	83–6,750
Black Vermillion River near Frankfort, KS (fig. 2, station no. 06885500)						
Log(SSC) = 0.829log(Turb) + 0.873	1.04	0.93	29%	15	59–3,611	264–5,900
Big Blue River near Manhattan, KS (fig. 2, station no. 06887000)						
Log(SSC) = 0.885log(Turb) + 0.262	1.01	0.86	19%	9	16–85	19–79

[1]Duan (1983).

[2]MSPE is root-mean-square error (a measure of the variance between regression-computed and measured values) expressed as a percentage.

[3]Turbidity values larger than 1,000 FNU were obtained using a simple regression to estimate in-stream YSI 6136 turbidity using Hach 2100AN turbidity data.

the Barnes, Marysville, and Frankfort streamgages were 0.12 lb/ft^3 (2.64 tons/acre-ft), 0.08 lb/ft^3 (1.76 tons/acre-ft), and 0.10 lb/ft^3 (2.19 tons/acre-ft).

The use of turbidity data in a regression model can provide more reliable and reproducible estimates of SSC and SSL than a regression model that uses discharge as the sole independent variable (Rasmussen and others, 2009). Case in point, the improved ability to estimate SSC and SSL using turbidity data was apparent in a comparison of turbidity-based and discharge-based SSC and SSL estimates for the Frankfort streamgage. The improvement afforded by the turbidity-based regression model was evidenced by the R^2 value of 0.93 as compared to the R^2 value of 0.66 for the discharge-based regression model (table 5). Further evidence of the improvement was provided by the MSPE (model standard percentage error), which was 29 percent for the turbidity-based model and

66 percent for the discharge-based model (table 5). MSPE is root-mean-square error (a measure of the variance between regression-computed and measured values) expressed as a percentage. The smaller the MSPE the less uncertain is the model (Helsel and Hirsch, 1992).

Use of the turbidity- and discharge-based regression models resulted in substantially different estimates of the total SSL at the Frankfort streamgage for the 2-year study period. Respectively, the turbidity- and discharge-based estimates of total SSL were 1.4 and 2.3 billion lb (table 5). Thus, use of discharge only to estimate SSC and SSL may result in over-prediction. Recently, Lee and others (2008), in a study of suspended-sediment transport for the Cottonwood and Neosho Rivers in east-central Kansas, also reported discharge-derived SSLs that were substantially larger than turbidity-derived SSLs.

Table 4. Suspended-sediment concentration, in-stream turbidity, discharge, percent silt/clay (less than 63 micrometers in diameter), and particle-size distribution from discrete samples collected at Kanopolis and Tuttle Creek Lake streamgage sites, 2008–10.

[Samples collected are equal-width increment samples unless otherwise noted. SSC, suspended-sediment concentration; mg/L, milligrams per liter; FNU, formazin nephelometric units; ft³/s, cubic feet per second; μm, micrometers; <, less than; --, not available; >, greater than]

Sample date (month/day/year)	SSC (mg/L)	In-stream turbidity[1] (FNU)	Discharge (ft³/s)	Percent of suspended-sediment (by weight) less than specified diameter (μm)						
				<100	<63	<31	<16	<8	<4	<2
Smoky Hill River at Ellsworth, KS (fig. 1, station no. 06864500)										
10/24/08	479	--	1,450	100	92	85	77	72	70	63
11/19/08	--	7.1	220	--	--	--	--	--	--	--
05/27/09	211	127	120	--	91	--	--	--	--	--
08/26/09	1,640	903	420	100	98	95	79	78	77	67
08/27/09	573	324	110	100	99	95	85	79	76	72
09/04/09	2,070	>1,000	740	100	97	91	72	63	59	51
03/05/10	40	19	70	--	--	--	--	--	--	--
03/28/10	301	134	150	--	97	--	--	--	--	--
05/20/10	2,020	975	1,290	100	95	88	71	60	48	38
05/20/10	1,480	826	980	100	96	88	78	68	60	52
05/21/10	462	271	460	100	96	91	82	75	59	47
05/26/10	2,200	>1,000	940	100	94	80	61	53	47	41
05/26/10	1,520	819	730	100	93	81	62	56	49	44
05/28/10	693	450	970	100	94	89	79	75	66	61
06/11/10	747	503	350	100	98	91	89	83	78	65
Smoky Hill River near Langley, KS (fig. 1, station no. 06865500)										
11/19/08	32	19	410	--	82	--	--	--	--	--
05/27/09	22	16	160	--	85	--	--	--	--	--
09/04/09	24	14	100	--	92	--	--	--	--	--
10/09/09	21	16	310	--	96	--	--	--	--	--
03/12/10	36	19	50	--	82	--	--	--	--	--
04/06/10	74	29	470	--	86	--	--	--	--	--
04/06/10	100	34	920	--	79	--	--	--	--	--
04/07/10	75	32	2,020	--	91	--	--	--	--	--
06/04/10	14	14	240	--	--	--	--	--	--	--
Big Blue River at Marysville, KS (fig. 2, station no. 06882510)										
10/15/08	1,420	--	4,620	100	97	83	60	46	43	39
10/23/08	2,180	--	5,070	100	92	71	47	35	34	31
04/27/09	4,870	>1,000	6,170	100	95	78	58	49	44	36
05/20/09	130	86	450	--	96	--	--	--	--	--
05/26/09	107	59	370	--	96	--	--	--	--	--
06/02/09	1,930	828	2,750	100	100	97	85	81	75	62
06/10/09	2,210	>1,000	2,450	100	99	96	85	78	74	64
06/16/09	4,770	>1,000	9,540	100	96	82	59	48	39	34
10/30/09	275	262	1,500	100	99	96	69	68	67	54
03/09/10	2,150	709	5,090	100	91	74	53	47	43	38
03/11/10	2,280	622	7,140	100	94	72	48	43	37	36
03/16/10	979	456	4,070	100	94	83	63	54	52	47
03/29/10	750	298	2,100	100	98	89	67	59	55	51
03/29/10	641	214	1,970	100	99	87	74	61	57	54
Little Blue River near Barnes, KS (fig. 2, station no. 06884400)										
10/15/08	2,590	794	3,580	100	77	63	44	32	32	31
10/23/08	2,630	907	12,000	100	75	64	48	39	37	33
04/27/09	6,750	>1,000	5,010	100	89	72	54	35	25	19

Table 4. Suspended-sediment concentration, in-stream turbidity, discharge, percent silt/clay (less than 63 micrometers in diameter), and particle-size distribution from discrete samples collected at Kanopolis and Tuttle Creek Lake streamgage sites, 2008–10.—Continued

[Samples collected are equal-width increment samples unless otherwise noted. SSC, suspended-sediment concentration; mg/L, milligrams per liter; FNU, formazin nephelometric units; ft³/s, cubic feet per second; μm, micrometers; <, less than; --, not available; >, greater than]

Sample date (month/day/year)	SSC (mg/L)	In-stream turbidity[1] (FNU)	Discharge (ft³/s)	Percent of suspended-sediment (by weight) less than specified diameter (μm)						
				<100	<63	<31	<16	<8	<4	<2
Little Blue River near Barnes, KS (fig. 2, station no. 06884400)—Continued										
05/20/09	83	21	240	--	96	--	--	--	--	--
06/02/09	462	270	380	100	96	86	80	69	68	65
06/03/09	2,030	840	960	100	91	82	64	55	53	49
11/02/09	287	209	370	100	92	89	82	73	62	58
03/09/10	1,890	579	2,080	100	85	64	45	39	36	34
03/09/10	2,370	735	2,280	100	86	73	52	46	42	37
03/10/10	2,940	800	2,920	100	75	59	43	39	36	33
03/11/10	4,790	>1,000	6,070	100	84	68	46	41	38	35
03/11/10	4,630	>1,000	6,070	100	81	73	54	49	42	39
03/30/10	1,060	430	1,180	100	90	79	66	57	53	50
03/30/10	943	393	1,130	100	92	78	67	61	56	52
04/30/10	5,370	>1,000	3,730	100	94	83	61	52	44	40
Black Vermillion River near Frankfort, KS (fig. 2, station no. 06885500)										
[2]10/15/08	1,770	--	3,000	--	94	--	--	--	--	--
10/23/08	513	--	350	100	98	97	83	68	61	55
03/24/09	5,900	>1,000	790	100	95	88	68	53	44	40
[2]04/27/09	3,500	>1,000	7,770	100	95	85	71	58	56	52
05/20/09	264	122	130	100	99	94	84	70	56	45
05/26/09	272	59	80	--	82	--	--	--	--	--
06/02/09	3,330	>1,000	6,390	100	95	89	67	56	51	45
06/10/09	1,780	718	730	100	91	82	66	57	54	50
06/16/09	2,750	>1,000	3,860	100	96	87	74	63	56	51
03/10/10	2,820	976	1,370	100	94	82	52	48	42	39
03/25/10	2,530	848	2,730	100	92	68	49	43	41	36
04/23/10	5,150	>1,000	3,330	100	89	73	48	37	35	33
04/23/10	4,780	>1,000	4,660	100	91	77	53	40	38	35
05/07/10	5,240	>1,000	1,470	100	94	78	57	46	40	36
05/21/10	1,090	374	1,080	100	92	78	51	48	46	43
Big Blue River near Manhattan, KS (fig. 2, station no. 06887000)										
[3]10/07/08	45	--	1,580	--	67	--	--	--	--	--
10/31/08	79	--	10,100	--	89	--	--	--	--	--
05/21/09	19	16	990	--	97	--	--	--	--	--
07/10/09	36	31	830	--	92	--	--	--	--	--
03/19/10	51	38	7,790	--	78	--	--	--	--	--
03/23/10	78	67	310	--	99	--	--	--	--	--
04/15/10	44	35	3,740	--	98	--	--	--	--	--
05/03/10	48	28	5,080	--	98	--	--	--	--	--
[3]05/06/10	69	23	6,000	--	51	--	--	--	--	--
08/09/10	23	24	12,600	--	--	--	--	--	--	--

[1]With one exception, turbidity values were measured using a YSI model 6136 sensor at a fixed location within the channel at each streamgage site. The exception was the Langley streamgage site for which turbidity was the median of cross-sectional measurements made during the collection of suspended-sediment samples.

[2]Single vertical sample.

[3]During the collection of this sample, some bed material may have been unintentionally included. Thus, the percent of suspended sediment less than 63 μm may not be representative.

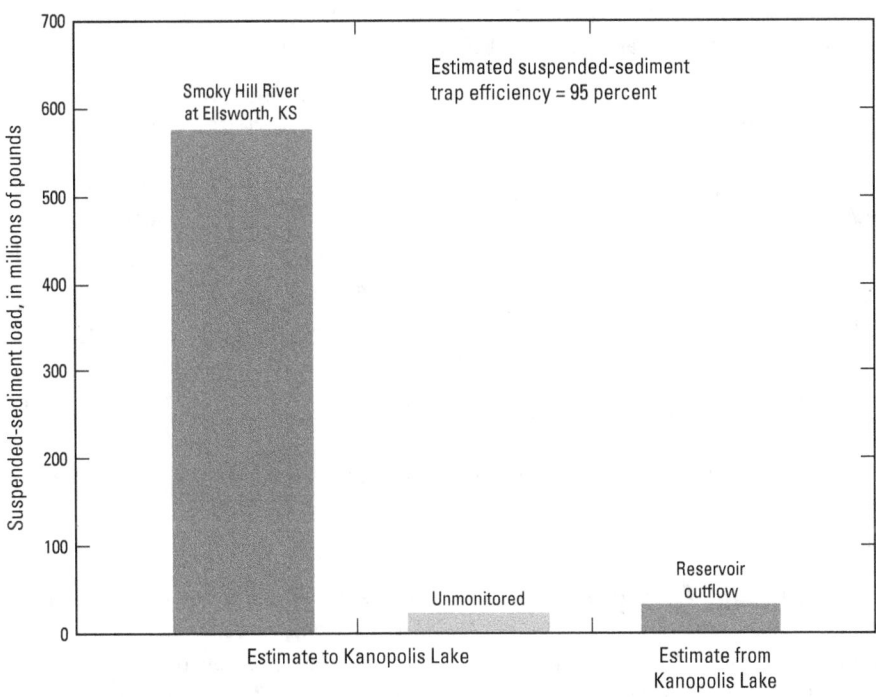

Figure 11. Approximate suspended-sediment load to and from Kanopolis Lake, October 1, 2008, to September 30, 2010.

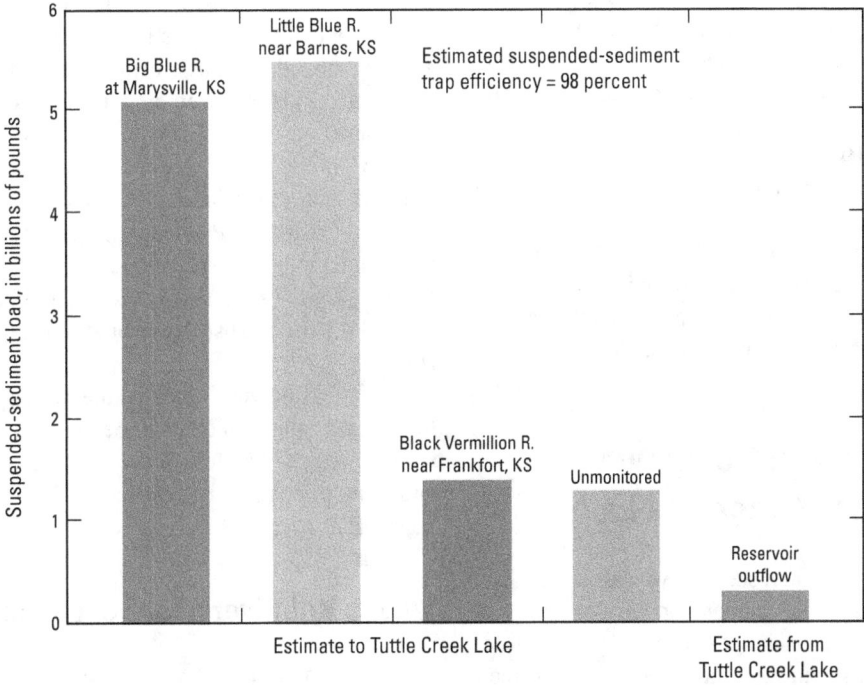

Figure 12. Approximate suspended-sediment load to and from Tuttle Creek Lake, October 1, 2008, to September 30, 2010.

Table 5. Comparison of turbidity-based and discharge-based regression models used to compute total suspended-sediment load at the Black Vermillion River near Frankfort streamgage (station 06885500), October 1, 2008, to September 30, 2010.

[R^2, coefficient of determination; MSPE, model standard percentage error; FNU, formazin nephelometric units; mg/L, milligrams per liter; SSL, suspended-sediment load; lbs, pounds; SSC, suspended-sediment concentration; Turb, turbidity; %, percent; Q, discharge in cubic feet per second]

Regression model	Duan bias correction[1]	R^2	Mean MSPE[2]	Number of samples	Range in turbidity (FNU)	Range in SSC (mg/L)	Estimated 2-year SSL (lbs)
Turbidity-based model							
Log(SSC) = 0.829log(Turb) + 0.873	1.04	0.93	29%	15	59–3,611	264–5,900	1.4 billion
Discharge-based model							
Log(SSC) = 0.616log(Q) + 1.358	1.22	0.66	66%	15	59–3,611	264–5,900	2.3 billion

[1]Duan (1983).

[2]MSPE is root-mean-square error (a measure of the variance between regression-computed and measured values) expressed as a percentage.

Stormflow Effects on Sediment Transport

In general, most of the SSL transport for a given year occurs during high-discharge periods (Meade and Parker, 1985; Morris and Fan, 1998; Lee and others, 2008). This pattern was evident in the present study. For example, at the Ellsworth streamgage for water year 2010, seven storms accounted for about 48 percent of the total discharge and about 88 percent of the total SSL (in 12 percent of the time). The largest stormflow (May 26 to June 5, 2010) during the year accounted for about 13 percent of the total discharge and about 26 percent of the total SSL (in 3 percent of the time).

At the Barnes streamgage for water year 2010, 14 storms accounted for about 72 percent of the total discharge and about 94 percent of the total SSL (in 30 percent of the time). The largest stormflow (June 19 to July 4, 2010) during the year accounted for about 24 percent of the total discharge and about 39 percent of the total SSL (in 4 percent of the time). This stormflow event had a peak discharge of almost 24,000 ft³/s with an estimated peak-streamflow recurrence interval of about once every 7 years (or an annual peak-streamflow probability of about 14 percent) (Perry and others, 2004).

Channel Stability Upstream and Downstream from Kanopolis Lake

For Kanopolis Lake, channel stability was assessed at five upstream streamgage sites and one downstream streamgage site. Analyses of discharge-width relations for the period of record for each streamgage indicated no pronounced changes in channel width. Several possible explanations may account for the apparent lack of channel-width change. First, channel width essentially was stable for the period of record at each streamgage site. Second, for a given site, channel width may have changed but the amount of change was less than what the analyses were able to detect. Third, the locations

where substantial channel-width change occurred (if any) were different from where the discharge-width data were collected. For example, high-flow discharge measurements typically are made at a bridge, whereas the locations of channel-width change may be upstream or downstream from the bridge. A related complication is the fact that channel banks at and near bridges sometimes are stabilized with riprap. In such cases, channel widening upstream or downstream from the bridge may be unlikely at the bridge. Finally, it is important to understand that channel width may not change substantially at a site with time if erosion on one bank is offset by deposition on the opposite bank. This is the case for a stable river that is actively meandering, as erosion on the outer bank of a meander (cutbank) is balanced by deposition on the inner bank of a meander (point bar) (Leopold, 1994; Knighton, 1998).

Inspection of 2008 aerial photography indicated substantial widening of the Smoky Hill River channel immediately downstream from the Kanopolis Lake outflow. However, no channel widening was evident in the aerial photography for the Langley streamgage site (station 06865500) which is located 0.8 mi downstream from the Kanopolis Lake outflow (fig. 13).

In the following sections, the results of analyses to assess historical changes in channel-bed elevation are presented. The results presented include the type, magnitude, timing, rate, and trend of channel-bed elevation changes at each site, as appropriate.

Smoky Hill River near Schoenchen

The Smoky Hill River near Schoenchen streamgage (station 06862700, fig. 1, table 1) presently (2010) is located 0.5 mi west of Schoenchen, Kansas. From 1964 to 1985, the streamgage was located 3.8 river mi upstream from the present site. From 1964 to 1975, the reference stage (for 20 ft³/s) decreased from 3.50 to 2.85 ft. During this period, the channel bed may have degraded a total of 0.65 ft at an average

Figure 13. Aerial photograph of channel widening on the Smoky Hill River immediately downstream from the Kanopolis Lake outflow.

rate of about 0.03 ft/yr (fig. 14). For this period, a statistically significant negative trend was indicated (Spearman's rho = -0.81, two-sided p-value = 0.004). Because the site was affected by beaver activity, the cause of the inferred change in channel-bed elevation may be beaver-related. For example, the inferred change may represent the recovery of the channel bed to its original elevation following the wash out or removal of a beaver dam located downstream from the streamgage. A plausible scenario is that the beaver dam provided temporary base-level control that caused upstream channel-bed aggradation. Since 1975, the channel bed at this site was relatively stable as evidenced by the fact that the stage-discharge rating curve developed in 1975 was used until 1985. In 1985, the streamgage was relocated 1.2 river mi downstream in an attempt to avoid beaver activity.

The streamgage was located 2.6 river mi upstream from the present site from 1985 to 2004. During this period, the reference stage decreased from 3.5 to 2.9 ft. Thus, the channel bed may have degraded a total of 0.6 ft at an average rate of about 0.03 ft/yr (fig. 14). For this period, a statistically significant negative trend was indicated (Spearman's rho = -0.88, two-sided p-value = 0.008). Again, because this site also was affected by beaver activity, the cause of the inferred change in channel-bed elevation may be beaver-related. In 2004, the streamgage was relocated 2.6 river mi downstream in a second attempt to avoid beaver activity. Since 2004, changes in the reference stage were minor and indicated that the channel-bed elevation essentially was stable at the present site, which was not affected by beaver activity.

Smoky Hill River below Schoenchen

The Smoky Hill River below Schoenchen streamgage (station 06862850, fig.1, table 1) is located about 2 river mi downstream from the streamgage near Schoenchen. From 1981 to 2004, the reference stage (for 20 ft³/s) indicated a net increase of 1.15 ft. However, from 1984 to 2002, the reference stage varied within 0.25 ft of the mean value of 2.50 ft indicating that the channel-bed elevation was relatively stable (fig. 15). Since 2004, the channel bed at this site was relatively stable as evidenced by the fact that the stage-discharge rating curve developed in 2004 was still in use as of 2010. Beaver activity has been an issue at this site and may, at least in part, account for the conditions observed.

Big Creek near Hays

The Big Creek near Hays streamgage (station 06863500, fig. 1, table 1) has been in operation since 1947. However, from 1947 to 1965, the streamgage was located 0.7 stream mi downstream from the present (2010) site and had concrete control. Thus, an assessment of channel-bed elevation change was not possible for this period. From 1965 to 1998, the streamgage was located 13.2 stream mi downstream from the present site. During this period, the reference stage (for 30 ft³/s) varied within 0.35 ft of the mean value of 3.85 ft (fig. 16) and indicated that the channel-bed elevation was relatively stable. Stability of the channel bed also was indicated

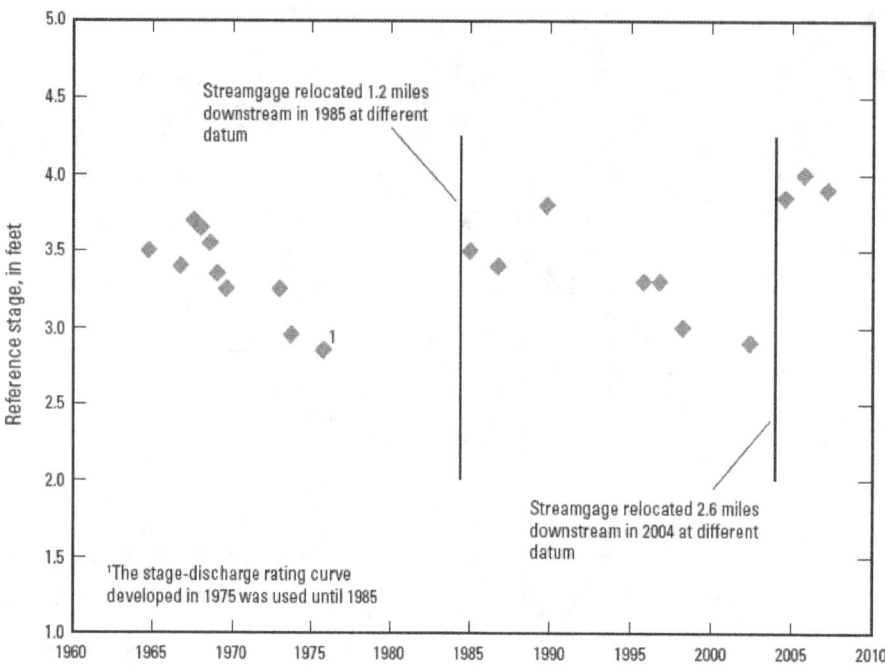

Figure 14.   Variation in stream stage for mean annual discharge (20 cubic feet per second) at Smoky Hill River near Schoenchen streamgage (station 06862700), 1964–2010.

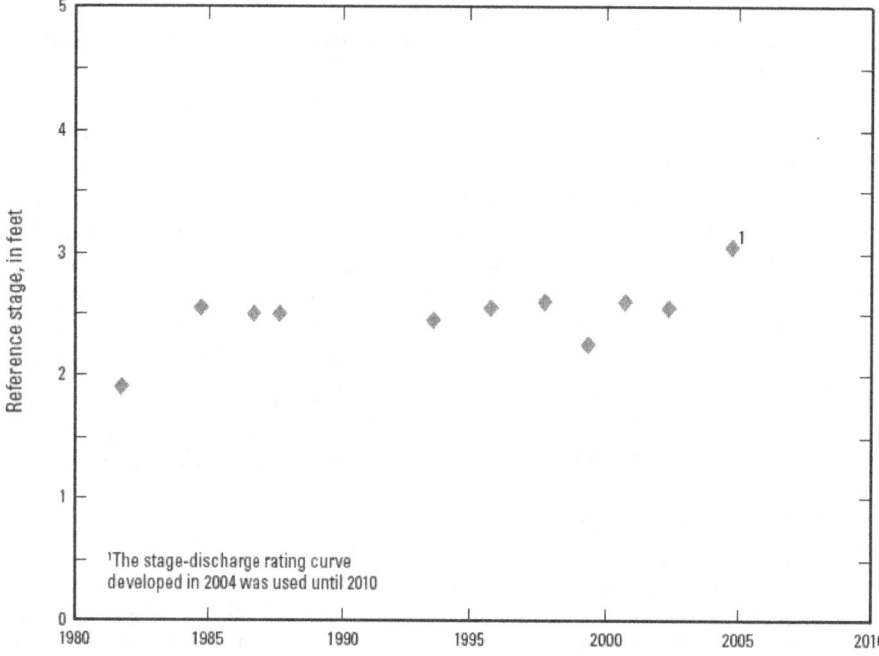

Figure 15.   Variation in stream stage for mean annual discharge (20 cubic feet per second) at Smoky Hill River below Schoenchen streamgage (station 06862850), 1981–2010.

by the fact that stage-discharge ratings developed in 1975 and 1986 were used for 9 and 10 years, respectively.

In 1998, the streamgage was relocated to its present site. Since 1998, changes in the reference stage were minor and indicated that the channel-bed elevation essentially was stable. The concrete control structure 0.7 stream mi downstream was still in place as of 2010. Basically, it is a weir that extends across the entire channel bed and rises about 3 ft above the downstream low-flow water surface. This structure provides base-level control that likely has some effect on the stability of the channel bed at the present streamgage site.

Smoky Hill River near Bunker Hill

The Smoky Hill River near Bunker Hill streamgage (station 06864050, fig. 1, table 1) is located about 43 river mi downstream from the "below Schoenchen" streamgage site. From 1939 to 1974, the streamgage was located 4.7 river mi upstream from the present (2010) site. During this period, the reference stage (for 150 ft^3/s) varied within 0.4 ft of the mean value of 3.0 ft (fig. 17). The channel-bed elevation appeared to be fluctuating in response to scour (erosion) and fill (deposition) processes that may reflect short-term changes in response to individual flow events. For example, a 0.5-ft decrease in reference stage on June 14, 1970, was caused by high flow that scoured the channel (D.L. Lacock, U.S. Geological Survey, written commun., 1971).

In 1974, the streamgage was relocated to its present site. Following an initial decrease, the reference stage varied within 0.25 ft of the mean value of 3.75 ft from 1981 to 2010 and indicated that the channel-bed elevation was relatively stable.

Smoky Hill River at Ellsworth

The Smoky Hill River at Ellsworth streamgage (station 06864500, fig. 1, table 1) is located about 48 river mi downstream from the "near Bunker Hill" streamgage site. From 1949 to about 1980, the reference stage (for 200 ft^3/s) steadily increased a net total of about 0.75 ft indicating that the channel bed slowly aggraded for about three decades (fig. 18). For this period, a statistically significant positive trend was indicated (Spearman's rho = 0.81, two-sided p-value < 0.001). The aggradation likely was a response to the artificial base level created downstream by Kanopolis Lake. Since 1980,

the reference stage varied within 0.25 ft of the mean value of 2.7 ft indicating that the channel-bed elevation was relatively stable. Throughout the period of record, fluctuations in the reference stage likely reflect short-term changes in channel-bed elevation caused by scour and fill processes associated with individual flow events.

Smoky Hill River near Langley

The Smoky Hill River near Langley streamgage (station 06865500, fig. 1, table 1) is located 0.8 river mi downstream from the Kanopolis Lake outflow. Between 1940 and the completion of the dam in 1948, the reference stage (for 300 ft^3/s) temporarily increased about 1 ft. (fig. 19). The increase indicated channel-bed deposition that may have been a result of the disturbance (and associated increased sediment load) caused by the construction of the dam. From 1948 to 1952, the reference stage decreased a total of 2.7 ft at a relatively rapid rate of about 0.7 ft/yr. For this period, a statistically significant negative trend was indicated (Spearman's rho = -0.96, two-sided p-value < 0.001). During the severe drought of the mid-1950s, the channel bed partially recovered as evidenced by a modest increase in the reference stage. Then, from 1957 to 2010, channel-bed degradation continued as evidenced by a 3.7-ft decrease in the reference stage at an average rate of about 0.07 ft/yr. For this period, a statistically significant negative trend was indicated (Spearman's rho = -1.0, two-sided p-value < 0.001). From 1948 to 2010, changes in the reference stage indicated that the channel bed at this site degraded a total of 6.15 ft. During this period the rate of degradation gradually decreased (fig. 19).

The long-term degradation of the channel bed at this site likely was caused, in large part, by the upstream presence of Kanopolis Lake (fig. 1). Reservoirs trap and permanently store much of the sediment load delivered from the upstream basin. For large reservoirs, the sediment trap efficiency typically is greater than 90 percent (Brune, 1953; Williams and Wolman, 1984; Shotbolt and others, 2005; Vanoni, 2006). In this study, the trap efficiency for Kanopolis Lake was estimated to be 95 percent. Downstream from the dam, an alluvial river typically will scour, and thus lower, its channel bed as the sediment-depleted water emerging from the spillway attempts to replenish its sediment load. Channel-bed erosion has been documented downstream from several large reservoirs in Kansas (Juracek, 2001).

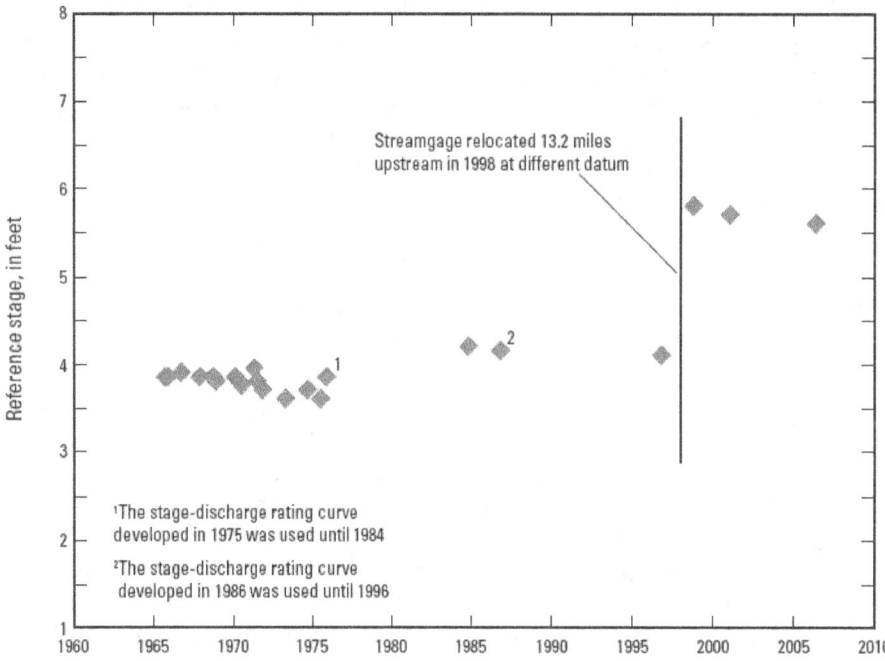

Figure 16. Variation in stream stage for mean annual discharge (30 cubic feet per second) at Big Creek near Hays streamgage (station 06863500), 1965–2010.

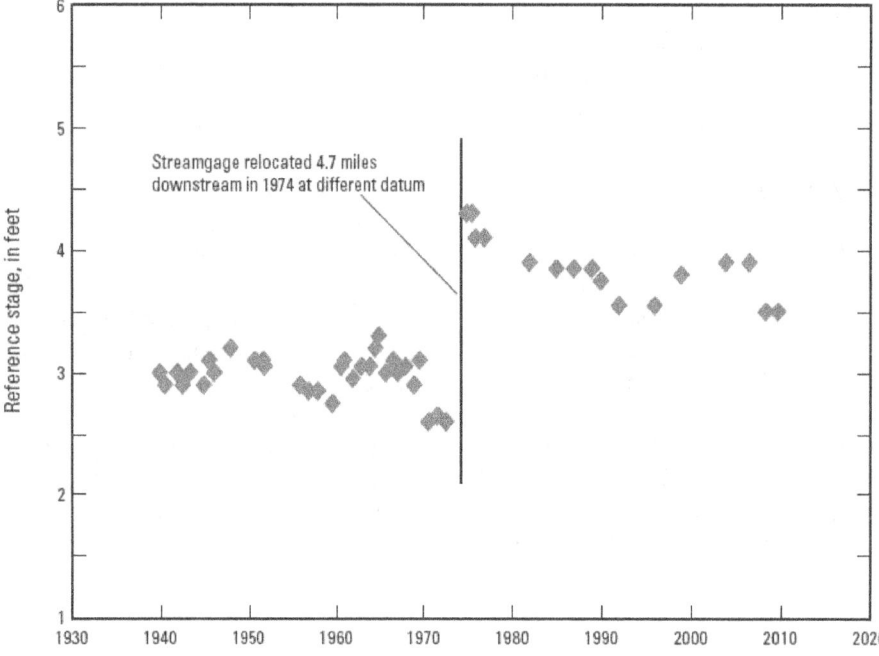

Figure 17. Variation in stream stage for mean annual discharge (150 cubic feet per second) at Smoky Hill River near Bunker Hill streamgage (station 06864050), 1939–2010.

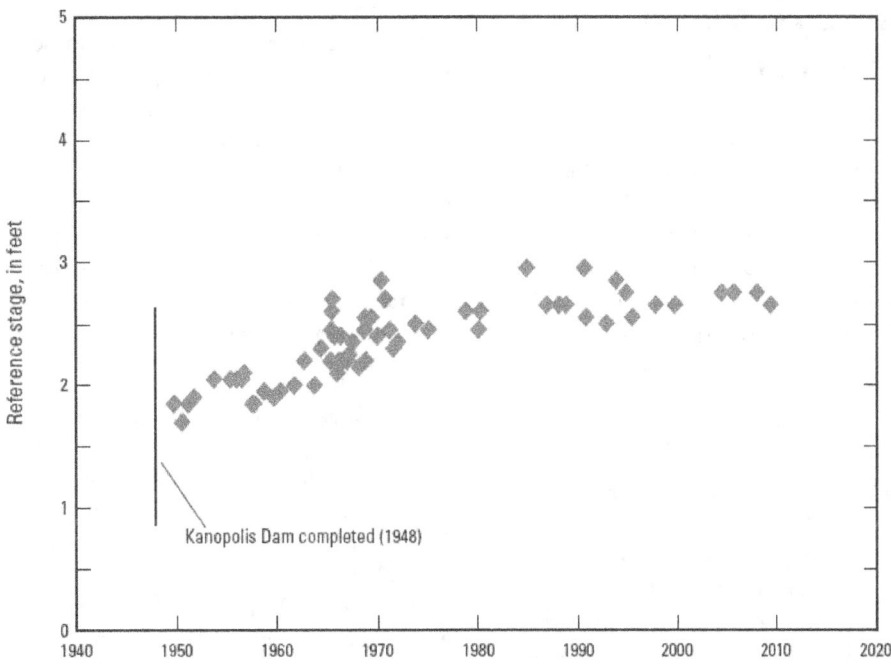

Figure 18. Variation in stream stage for mean annual discharge (200 cubic feet per second) at Smoky Hill River at Ellsworth streamgage (station 06864500), 1949–2010.

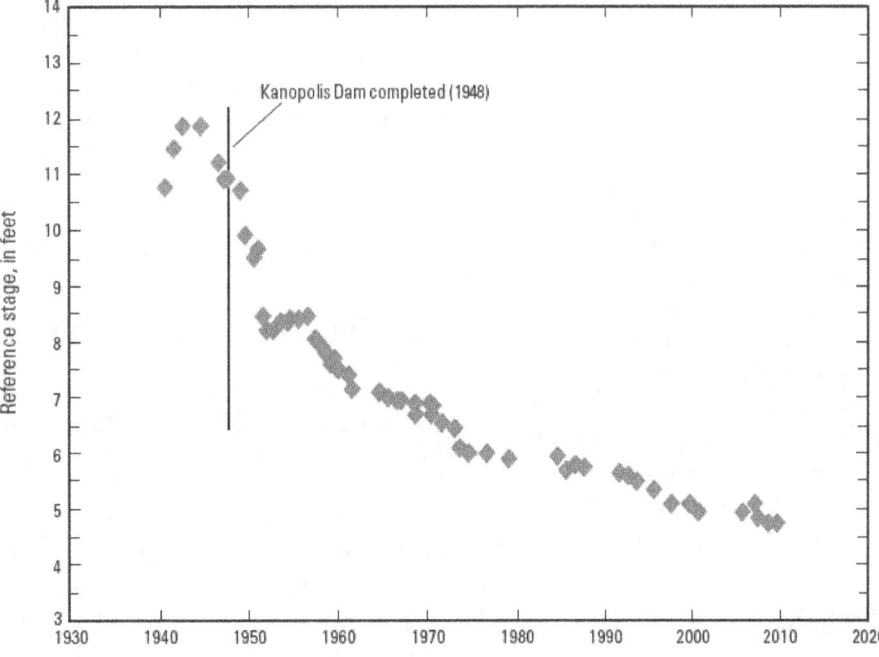

Figure 19. Variation in stream stage for mean annual discharge (300 cubic feet per second) at Smoky Hill River near Langley streamgage (station 06865500), 1940–2010.

Channel Stability Upstream and Downstream from Tuttle Creek Lake

For Tuttle Creek Lake, channel stability was assessed at six upstream streamgage sites and one downstream streamgage site. With the exception of possible widening at the Barnes streamgage site (station 06884400, fig. 2, table 1) in the 1980s, analyses of discharge-width relations for the period of record for each upstream streamgage indicated no pronounced changes in channel width. As described for the Kanopolis Lake streamgage sites, several possible explanations may account for the apparent lack of channel-width change.

About 2.5 river mi downstream from the Tuttle Creek Lake outflow, at the Manhattan streamgage site (station 06887000, fig. 2, table 1), channel widening was indicated. From July 20 to August 8, 1993, a sustained high-flow release from the dam included mean daily discharges that ranged from 25,000 to almost 60,000 ft³/s. In comparison, the mean annual discharge for this site (period of record 1963 to 2009) was about 2,300 ft³/s (U.S. Geological Survey, 2011). The sustained high flow widened the channel about 60 ft (30 percent) (fig. 20). During the high-flow release, the north abutment of the bridge was washed out at the streamgage site (Seth Studley, U.S. Geological Survey, oral commun., 2010). Since 1993, the widened channel has persisted to the present (2010).

In the following sections, the results of analyses to assess historical changes in channel-bed elevation are presented. The results presented include the type, magnitude, timing, rate, and trend of channel-bed elevation changes at each site, as appropriate.

Big Blue River at Marysville

The Big Blue River at Marysville streamgage (station 06882510, fig.2, table 1) has been in operation since 1984. From 1985 to 2004, the reference stage (for 1,000 ft³/s) decreased 1.15 ft at an average rate of about 0.06 ft/yr (fig. 21). For this period, a statistically significant negative trend was indicated (Spearman's rho = -0.94, two-sided p-value < 0.001). The 0.55-ft increase in reference stage in 1987 possibly was related to substantial bank slumping that occurred that year (J.E. Putnam, U.S. Geological Survey, written commun., 1988). From 2004 to 2010, minimal change in the reference stage indicated that the channel bed was stable.

Mill Creek at Washington

The Mill Creek at Washington streamgage (station 06884200, fig. 2, table 1) has been in operation since 1959. From 1959 to 2010, the reference stage (for 100 ft³/s) decreased 1 ft (fig. 22). For this period, a statistically significant negative trend (Spearman's rho = -0.48, two-sided p-value = 0.003) indicated overall channel-bed degradation. However, during this period, pronounced fluctuations in the reference stage provided evidence for multiple changes in channel-bed elevation likely in response to short-term scour and fill processes. For example, high flows and associated bank slumping were responsible for the pronounced increases in reference stage that occurred in 1973 (R.E. Curtis, U.S. Geological Survey, written commun., 1974) and 1983 (J. Marshall, U.S. Geological Survey, written commun., 1984). Substantial channel-bed deposits apparently were removed quickly by erosion as evidenced by multiple sequences in which a pronounced increase in reference stage was immediately followed by a pronounced decrease in reference stage (fig. 22).

Little Blue River near Barnes

The Little Blue River near Barnes streamgage (station 06884400, fig. 2, table 1) is presently (2010) located about 10 river mi upstream from the confluence with the Big Blue River. Until 2004, the streamgage was located 6.5 river mi upstream from the present site. From 1958 to 1976, the reference stage (for 700 ft³/s) varied within 0.55 ft of the mean value of 4.8 ft (fig. 23). From 1976 to 1984, the channel bed was relatively stable as evidenced by the fact that the stage-discharge rating curve developed in 1976 was used throughout the period. In June 1984, the reference stage increased 0.75 ft. The increase indicated deposition of material on the channel bed that likely was associated with a high flow that occurred at that time (U.S. Geological Survey, 2011). From 1984 to 1998, the reference stage decreased from 5.7 to 4.2 ft at an average rate of about 0.11 ft/yr. For this period, a statistically significant negative trend (Spearman's rho = -0.95, two-sided p-value < 0.001) indicated channel-bed degradation. A constant reference stage indicated that the channel bed was stable from 1998 to 2003. In 2004, the streamgage was relocated to the present site. From 2004 to 2010, the reference stage fluctuated within 0.15 ft of the mean value of 5.4 ft and indicated that the channel bed was relatively stable.

Little Blue River at Waterville

The Little Blue River at Waterville streamgage (station 06884500, fig. 2, table 1) was located 5 river mi downstream from the present Barnes streamgage and 5 river mi upstream from the confluence with the Big Blue River. With the exception of a 0.3 ft increase in the reference stage (for 600 ft³/s) in 1935 that likely was associated with a high flow in April 1935 (J.B. Spiegel, U.S. Geological Survey, written commun., 1936), the reference stage varied minimally from 1929 to 1942 and indicated that the channel bed was relatively stable (fig. 24). In 1943, the reference stage increased 1.8 ft. The increase indicated deposition of material on the channel bed that likely was associated with a high flow in June 1943 (J.B. Spiegel, U.S. Geological Survey, written commun., 1944). From 1943 to 1953, the reference stage varied considerably indicating changes in channel-bed elevation that likely were in response to short-term scour and fill processes.

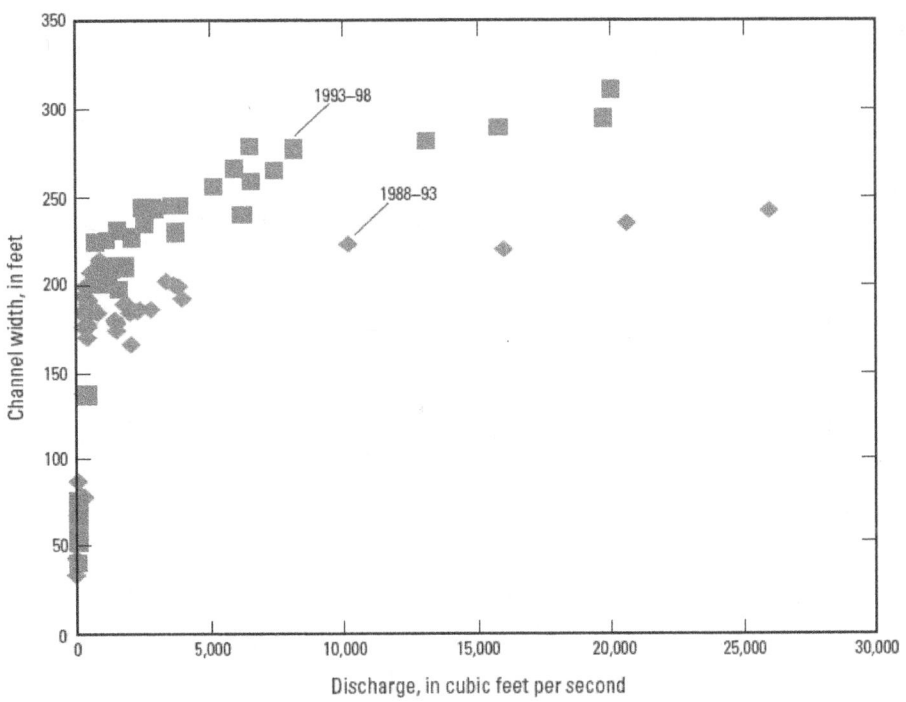

Figure 20. Relation between discharge and channel width at Big Blue River near Manhattan streamgage (station 06887000).

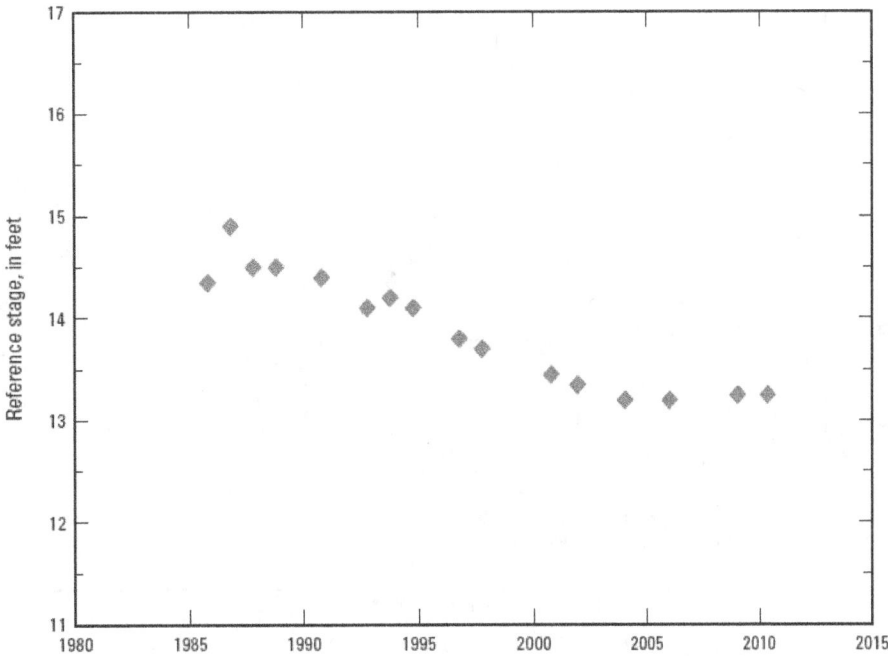

Figure 21. Variation in stream stage for mean annual discharge (1,000 cubic feet per second) at Big Blue River at Marysville streamgage (station 06882510), 1985–2010.

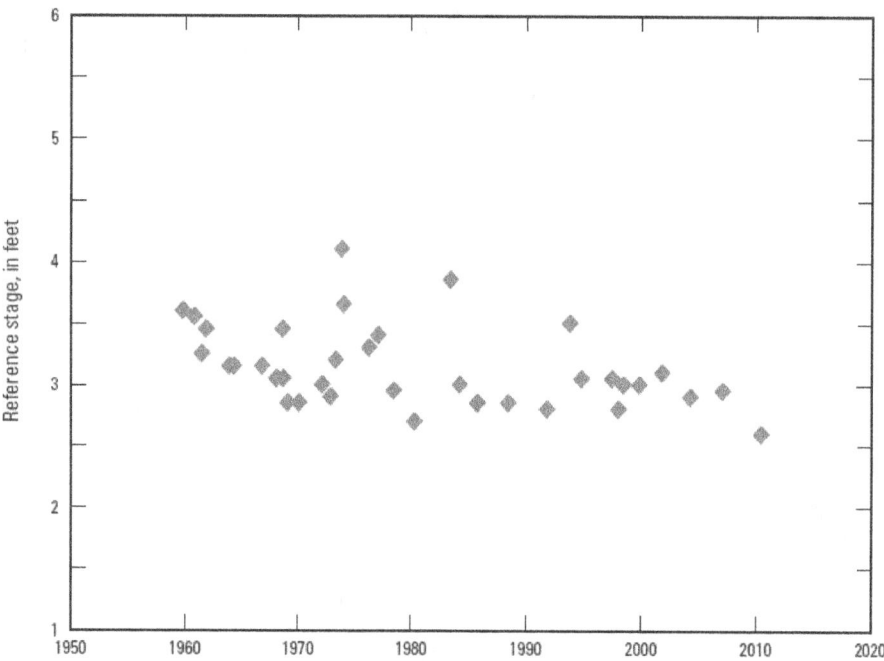

Figure 22. Variation in stream stage for mean annual discharge (100 cubic feet per second) at Mill Creek at Washington streamgage (station 06884200), 1959–2010.

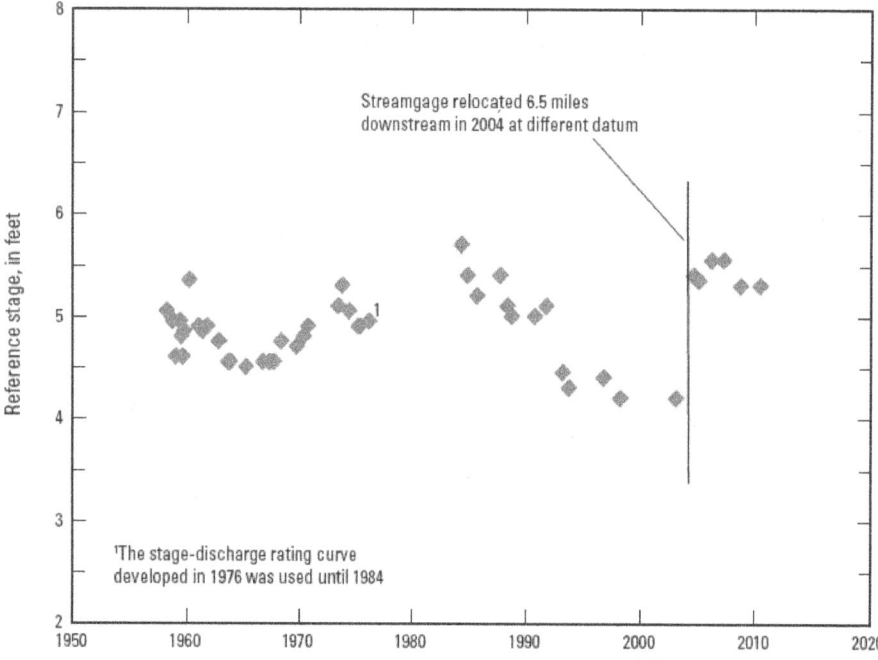

Figure 23. Variation in stream stage for mean annual discharge (700 cubic feet per second) at Little Blue River near Barnes streamgage (station 06884400), 1958–2010.

Minimal change in the reference stage from 1954 to 1958 indicated that the channel-bed stabilized during the drought of the mid-1950s.

Black Vermillion River near Frankfort

The Black Vermillion River near Frankfort streamgage (station 06885500, fig. 2, table 1) is located about 19 river mi upstream from the confluence with the Big Blue River. From 1953 to 1964, the reference stage (for 150 ft³/s) varied within 0.5 ft of the mean value of 6.0 ft (fig. 25). The variability in the reference stage indicated changes in channel-bed elevation that likely were in response to short-term scour and fill processes. The channel bed was stable from 1964 to 1969 as indicated by no change in the reference stage. From 1969 to 1989, the reference stage increased from 5.65 to 7.3 ft at an average rate of about 0.08 ft/yr. For this period, a statistically significant positive trend (Spearman's rho = 0.89, two-sided p-value < 0.001) indicated channel-bed aggradation. From 1989 to 2010, the reference stage decreased from 7.3 to 4.9 ft at an average rate of about 0.11 ft/yr. For this period, a statistically significant negative trend (Spearman's rho = -0.95, two-sided p-value < 0.001) indicated channel-bed degradation.

The documented aggradational trend (1969–1989) and subsequent degradational trend (1989–2010) at the streamgage site may be indicative of the passage of a sediment pulse that originated from disturbed areas upstream in the Black Vermillion River Basin. Meade (2009), in a comparison of channel depths at 56 sites in the basin surveyed in 1963 and 2008, determined that channels deepened an average of about 5 ft. Widespread channelization in the basin likely was a contributing factor. Channelization results in channel shortening that increases channel slope and flow velocity. A typical geomorphic response to channelization is substantial channel degradation upstream that ultimately may affect the entire drainage system. In addition, channel aggradation may occur downstream (Simon and Rinaldi, 2006).

Big Blue River at Randolph

The Big Blue River at Randolph streamgage (station 06886000, fig. 2, table 1) was located about 0.5 river mi upstream from the confluence with Fancy Creek. From 1929 to 1935, the reference stage (for 2,000 ft³/s) varied within 0.05 ft of the mean value of 5.7 ft indicating that the channel-bed elevation was essentially stable (fig. 26). In early 1936, the reference stage increased 0.45 ft to 6.1 ft. The cause of this increase could not be determined with certainty. A plausible explanation is deposition of material at, and downstream from, the streamgage site the sources of which were the Big Blue River and Fancy Creek. Backwater from Fancy Creek, and associated deposition in the Big Blue River channel at the mouth of Fancy Creek, was noted on occasion (H.P. Brooks, U.S. Geological Survey, written commun., 1941; R.E. Curtis, Jr., U.S. Geological Survey, written commun., 1959). Deposition at the mouth of Fancy Creek may have caused deposition upstream in the Big Blue River channel in the vicinity of the streamgage site.

Subsequent changes in the reference stage from 1936 through 1960 indicated that the material presumably deposited in early 1936 was resistant to erosion. The basis for this interpretation was the fact that, although the reference stage fluctuated considerably during that period, it frequently reached but never dropped below 6.1 ft (fig. 26). The fluctuations in reference stage indicated changes in channel-bed elevation likely caused by short-term scour and fill processes. The 1.25-ft increase in the reference stage in 1951 was associated with a high flow in May 1951 (E.J. Kennedy, U.S. Geological Survey, written commun., 1953).

Big Blue River near Manhattan

The Big Blue River near Manhattan streamgage (station 06887000, fig. 2, table 1) is located 2.5 river mi downstream from the Tuttle Creek Lake outflow. Although the reservoir was officially completed in 1962 by USACE, water storage actually began in 1959. From 1953 to 1960, the reference stage (for 2,500 ft³/s) varied within 0.5 ft of the mean value of 8.3 ft and indicated that the channel-bed elevation was relatively stable (fig. 27). During this period, increases in reference stage may, in part, have been a result of the disturbance (and associated increased sediment load) caused by the construction of the dam. From 1960 to 1998, the reference stage decreased from 8.4 to 4.2 ft at an average rate of about 0.11 ft/yr. For this period, a statistically significant negative trend (Spearman's rho = -0.98, two-sided p-value < 0.001) indicated channel-bed degradation. The long-term degradation of the channel bed at this site likely was caused, in large part, by the upstream release of sediment-depleted water from Tuttle Creek Lake. The anomalous 0.7-ft increase in the reference stage in 1967 was caused by bank slumping associated with a large release from Tuttle Creek Lake in June 1967 (J.D. Craig, U.S. Geological Survey, written commun., 1968). From 1998 to 2010, the reference stage varied within 0.25 ft of the mean value of 4.4 ft and indicated that the channel-bed elevation was relatively stable.

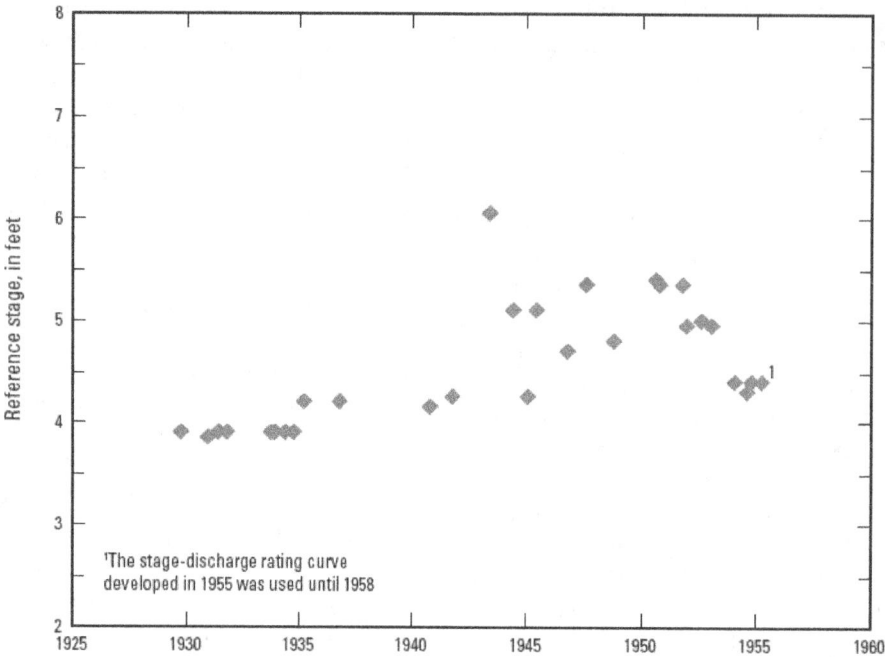

Figure 24. Variation in stream stage for mean annual discharge (600 cubic feet per second) at Little Blue River at Waterville streamgage (station 06884500), 1929–1958.

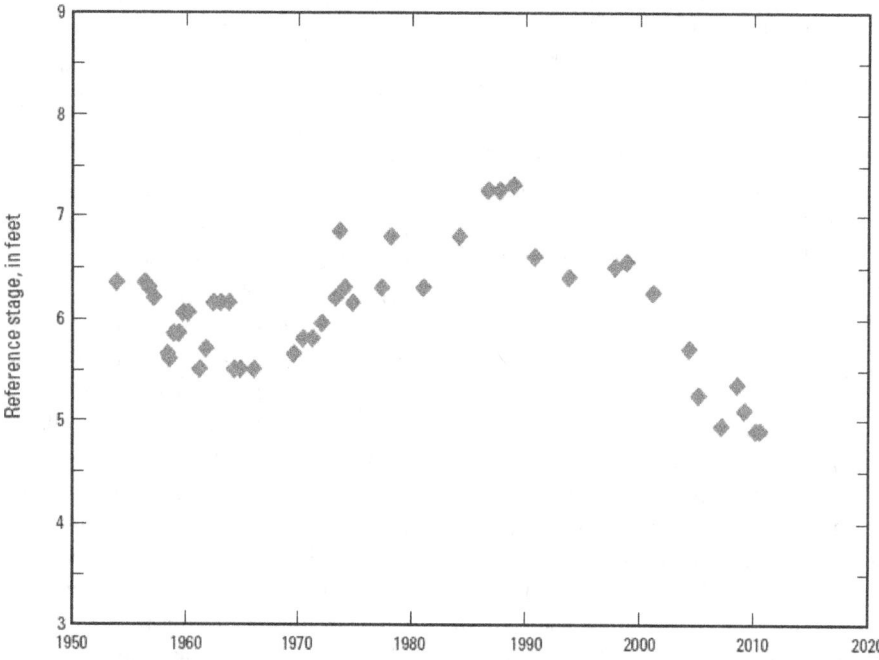

Figure 25. Variation in stream stage for mean annual discharge (150 cubic feet per second) at Black Vermillion River near Frankfort streamgage (station 06885500), 1953–2010.

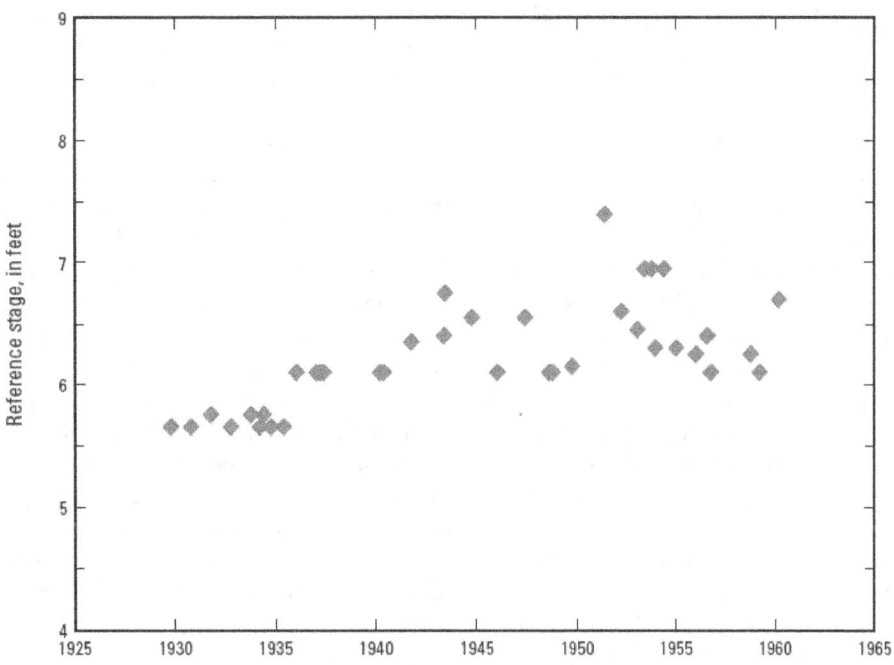

Figure 26.   Variation in stream stage for mean annual discharge (2,000 cubic feet per second) at Big Blue River at Randolph streamgage (station 06886000), 1929–1960.

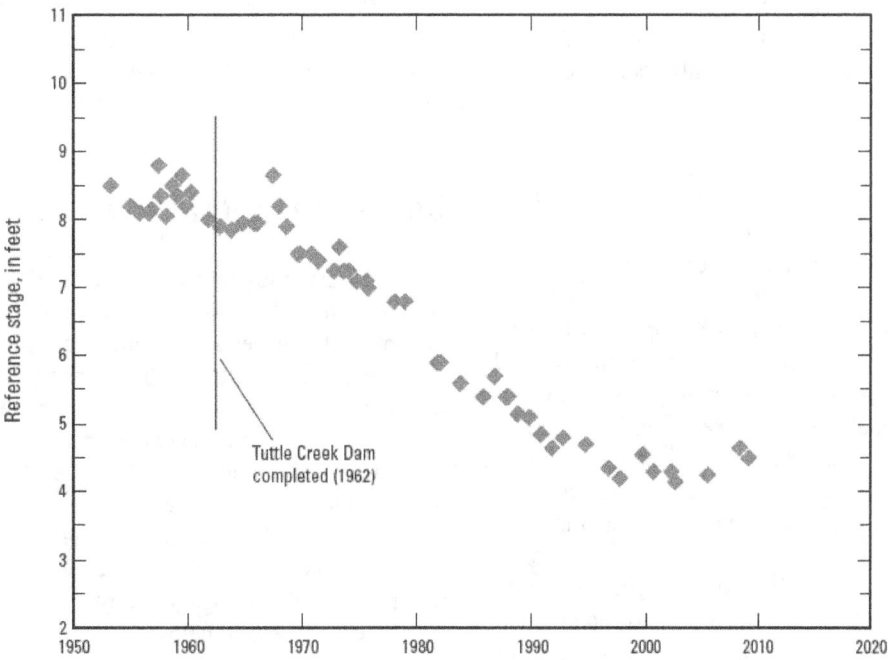

Figure 27.   Variation in stream stage for mean annual discharge (2,500 cubic feet per second) at Big Blue River near Manhattan streamgage (station 06887000), 1953–2010.

Sediment Sources for Kanopolis and Tuttle Creek Lakes

An effective management plan to reduce the sediment loads delivered to Kanopolis and Tuttle Creek Lakes requires an understanding of the type and relative importance of various sediment sources (Collins and Walling, 2004; Walling, 2005). In this discussion, sediment refers to silt and clay because particle-size analyses of core samples determined that the bottom sediment deposited in the reservoirs was predominantly silt and clay. Specifically, the silt and clay content of the Kanopolis Lake bottom sediment averaged 87 percent (Kansas Biological Survey, 2009) whereas the silt and clay content of the Tuttle Creek Lake bottom sediment typically was 98 percent or greater (Juracek and Mau, 2002). Likewise, the particle-size composition of the suspended-sediment samples collected at the inflow streamgage sites also was predominantly silt and clay. The median percentage of silt and clay for samples collected at the Ellsworth, Barnes, Frankfort, and Marysville streamgage sites was 96, 89, 94, and 96 percent, respectively (table 4).

The sediment deposited in the reservoirs mostly originates from four possible sources. Three of the sources are upstream from the reservoirs and include channel beds, channel banks, and surface soils within the basins (Waters, 1995). The fourth source is the shoreline surrounding each reservoir (Morris and Fan, 1998). Any of these four sources potentially may contribute a substantial amount of sediment to the reservoirs. The importance of surface soils and shoreline as sediment sources was not specifically addressed in this study. Atmospheric deposition was assumed to be relatively insignificant.

Channel beds are not considered to be a major present-day (2010) source of sediment to the reservoirs. In order for channel beds to be a true source, pronounced bed degradation would be required. With the possible exception of the "near Schoenchen" streamgage site (which has stabilized), long-term channel-bed degradation upstream from Kanopolis Lake was not indicated at the streamgage sites. Instead, the channel beds generally appeared to be serving as temporary storage locations (for example, for material introduced from bank slumping or erosion of surface soils) from which deposited sediment is subsequently remobilized and transported downstream. Channel-bed degradation for some distance upstream from Kanopolis Lake is unlikely because the reservoir provides base-level control. In fact, at the Ellsworth streamgage site (fig. 1), long-term channel-bed aggradation followed by relative stability was indicated (fig. 18). Upstream from Tuttle Creek Lake, long-term channel-bed degradation was indicated at the Marysville (fig. 21) and Frankfort (fig. 25) streamgage sites. However, at the Marysville site the channel bed has stabilized. At the Frankfort site the degradation may, in part, represent the removal of previous deposits rather than erosion of the pre-deposit channel bed. Pronounced channel-bed degradation was not indicated at the other streamgage sites

upstream from Tuttle Creek Lake. Because of the base-level control provided by the reservoir, channel-bed degradation is unlikely for some distance upstream from Tuttle Creek Lake.

Channel banks likely are a substantial source of sediment to the reservoirs. The combined evidence of aerial photographs, onsite inspections, and USGS streamgage information indicated that bank erosion is an active and ongoing process upstream from the reservoirs. Multiple sites of currently (2010) or recently (2005-2008) active bank erosion were identified on aerial photographs and during onsite inspections. Historical USGS streamgage information documented bank slumps that occurred in the vicinity of some streamgages.

For both reservoirs, the relative importance (that is, in terms of the amount of sediment contributed) of the four sediment sources is uncertain. Determination of the relative importance of sediment sources may be possible using chemical tracers or other methods. For example, in a recent study of Perry Lake, Kansas (fig. 2), chemical tracers were used to determine that channel banks were more important than surface soils as sediment sources for the reservoir (Juracek and Ziegler, 2009).

As part of an overall understanding of sediment sources, it is important to keep three considerations in mind. First, sediment yield can vary substantially throughout a basin and a small percentage of a basin can account for a large percentage of the sediment yield (Morris and Fan, 1998; Russell and others, 2001; Lee and others, 2009). Second, the contribution of sediment from channel erosion tends to become more important with distance downstream in a basin (Knighton, 1998; Lawler and others, 1999; Walling, 2005; Juracek and Ziegler, 2009). Finally, the relative contribution of various sediment sources likely will change with time.

Summary and Conclusions

A 3-year study by the U.S. Geological Survey, in cooperation with the Kansas Water Office, was begun in 2008 to determine the suspended-sediment load delivered to Kanopolis and Tuttle Creek Lakes, the amount of suspended sediment retained in each reservoir, and river channel stability upstream and downstream from the reservoirs. Suspended-sediment loads delivered to and released from each reservoir were computed using continuous streamflow and turbidity data collected at upstream and downstream streamgage sites from October 1, 2008, to September 30, 2010. Channel stability was assessed using historical streamgage information. The results of this study are summarized below:

1. The total 2-year inflow SSL to Kanopolis Lake was computed to be 600 million lb.

2. The total 2-year outflow SSL from Kanopolis Lake was computed to be 31 million lb.

3. Sediment trap efficiency for Kanopolis Lake was estimated to be 95 percent.

4. The total 2-year inflow SSL to Tuttle Creek Lake was computed to be 13.3 billion lb.

5. The total 2-year outflow SSL from Tuttle Creek Lake was computed to be 327 million lb.

6. Sediment trap efficiency for Tuttle Creek Lake was estimated to be 98 percent.

7. The mean annual suspended-sediment yields from the Kanopolis and Tuttle Creek Lake Basins were estimated to be 129,000 lb/mi²/yr and 691,000 lb/mi²/yr, respectively.

8. For both reservoirs, most of the inflow suspended-sediment load was delivered during short-term, high-discharge periods.

9. For the purpose of computing suspended-sediment concentration and load, the use of turbidity data in a regression model can provide more reliable and reproducible estimates than a regression model that uses discharge as the sole independent variable. Moreover, the use of discharge only to compute suspended-sediment concentration and load may result in overprediction.

10. In general, no pronounced channel-width changes were evident at the streamgage sites located upstream from Kanopolis and Tuttle Creek Lakes.

11. At the Ellsworth streamgage site, located upstream from Kanopolis Lake, long-term channel-bed aggradation followed by stability was indicated.

12. At the Langley streamgage site, located immediately downstream from Kanopolis Lake, the channel bed degraded 6.15 ft from 1948 to 2010.

13. At the Barnes and Marysville streamgage sites, located upstream from Tuttle Creek Lake, long-term channel-bed degradation followed by stability was indicated.

14. At the Frankfort streamgage site, located upstream from Tuttle Creek Lake, channel-bed aggradation of 1.65 ft from 1969 to 1989 followed by channel-bed degradation of 2.4 ft from 1989 to 2010 was indicated. These pronounced changes may represent the passage of a sediment pulse caused by historical disturbances (for example, channelization) in the upstream basin.

15. With the exception of the Frankfort streamgage site, current (2010) conditions at the streamgages located upstream from Kanopolis and Tuttle Creek Lakes were typified by channel-bed stability.

16. At the Manhattan streamgage site, located downstream from Tuttle Creek Lake, high-flow releases associated with the 1993 flood widened the channel about 60 ft (30 percent).

17. At the Manhattan streamgage site, the channel bed degraded 4.2 ft from 1960 to 1998. Since 1998, the channel bed has been relatively stable.

18. Stream channel banks, compared to channel beds, likely are a more important source of sediment to Kanopolis and Tuttle Creek Lakes from the upstream basins.

References Cited

Brune, G.M., 1953, Trap efficiency of reservoirs: Transactions of the American Geophysical Union, v. 34, p. 407–448.

Collins, A.L., and Walling, D.E., 2004, Documenting catchment suspended sediment sources—Problems, approaches and prospects: Progress in Physical Geography, v. 28, p. 159–196.

Duan, Naihua, 1983, Smearing estimate—A nonparametric retransformation method: Journal of the American Statistical Association, v. 78, p. 605–610.

Fenneman, N.M., 1946, Physical divisions of the United States: U.S. Geological Survey special map, scale 1:7,000,000, 1 sheet.

Guy, H.P., 1969, Laboratory theory and methods for sediment analysis: U.S. Geological Survey Techniques of Water-Resources Investigations, book 5, chap. C1, 58 p.

Hach Company, 2000, Model 2100AN laboratory turbidimeter: accessed January 25, 2011, at *http://www.hach.com/*.

Hach Company, 2005, SOLITAX sc turbidity and suspended solids sensors: accessed October 4, 2010, at *http://www.hach.com/*.

Helsel, D.R., and Hirsch, R.M., 1992, Statistical methods in water resources: Amsterdam, Elsevier Science Publishers, 529 p.

High Plains Regional Climate Center, 2010, Historical climate data summaries: Information available on the Web, accessed October 4, 2010, at *http://www.hprcc.unl.edu/*.

Jordan, P.R., and Stamer, J.K., eds., 1995, Surface-water-quality assessment of the lower Kansas River Basin, Kansas and Nebraska—Analysis of available data through 1986: U.S. Geological Survey Water-Supply Paper 2352–B, 161 p.

Juracek, K.E., 2001, Channel-bed elevation changes downstream from large reservoirs in Kansas: U.S. Geological Survey Water-Resources Investigations Report 01–4205, 24 p.

Juracek, K.E., 2004, Historical channel-bed elevation change as a result of multiple disturbances, Soldier Creek, Kansas: Physical Geography, v. 25, p. 269–290.

Juracek, K.E., and Mau, D.P., 2002, Sediment deposition and occurrence of selected nutrients and other chemical constituents in bottom sediment, Tuttle Creek Lake, northeast Kansas, 1962–99: U.S. Geological Survey Water-Resources Investigations Report 02–4048, 73 p.

Juracek, K.E., and Fitzpatrick, F.A., 2009, Geomorphic applications of stream-gage information: River Research and Applications, v. 25, p. 329–347.

Juracek, K.E., and Ziegler, A.C., 2009, Estimation of sediment sources using selected chemical tracers in the Perry Lake Basin, Kansas, USA: International Journal of Sediment Research, v. 24, p. 108–125.

Kansas Applied Remote Sensing Program, 2009, 2005 Kansas land cover patterns, scale 1:50,000: accessed October 2010 at *http://www.kansasgis.org.*

Kansas Biological Survey, 2009, Bathymetric and sediment survey of Kanopolis Reservoir, Ellsworth County, Kansas: Kansas Biological Survey report 2008–09, 26 p.

Kansas Department of Health and Environment, 2010, 303(d) methodology and list: accessed September 30, 2010, at *http://www.kdheks.gov/tmdl/methodology.htm.*

Kansas Water Office, 2010a, Kanopolis Lake, Reservoir information sheet: accessed September 30, 2010, at *http://www.kwo.org/reservoirs/Reservoirs.htm.*

Kansas Water Office, 2010b, Tuttle Creek Lake, Reservoir information sheet: accessed September 30, 2010, at *http://www.kwo.org/reservoirs/Reservoirs.htm.*

Kennedy, E.J., 1983, Computation of continuous records of streamflow: U.S. Geological Survey Techniques of Water-Resources Investigations, book 3, chap. A13, 53 p.

Kennedy, E.J., 1984, Discharge ratings at gaging stations: U.S. Geological Survey Techniques of Water-Resources Investigations, book 3, chap. A10, 59 p.

Knighton, D., 1998, Fluvial forms and processes—A new perspective: New York, John Wiley and Sons, 383 p.

Lawler, D.M., Grove, J.R., Couperthwaite, J.S., and Leeks, G.J.L., 1999, Downstream change in river bank erosion rates in the Swale-Ouse system, northern England: Hydrological Processes, v. 13, p. 977–992.

Lee, C.J., Rasmussen, P.P., and Ziegler, A.C., 2008, Characterization of suspended-sediment loading to and from John Redmond Reservoir, east-central Kansas, 2007–2008: U.S. Geological Survey Scientific Investigations Report 2008–5123, 25 p.

Lee, C.J., Rasmussen, P.P., Ziegler, A.C., and Fuller, C.C., 2009, Transport and sources of suspended sediment in the Mill Creek Watershed, Johnson County, northeast Kansas, 2006–07: U.S. Geological Survey Scientific Investigations Report 2009–5001, 52 p.

Leopold, L.B., 1994, A view of the river: Cambridge, Massachusetts, Harvard University Press, 298 p.

Meade, B.K., 2009, Spatial extent, timing, and causes of channel incision, Black Vermillion watershed, northeastern Kansas: Manhattan, Kansas, Kansas State University, M.A. thesis, 173 p.

Meade, R.H., and Parker, R.S., 1985, Sediment in rivers of the United States: National Water Summary 1984, U.S. Geological Survey Water-Supply Paper 2275, p. 49–60.

Morris, G.L., and Fan, Jiahua, 1998, Reservoir sedimentation handbook: New York, McGraw-Hill, various pagination.

Nolan, K.M., Gray, J.R., and Glysson, G.D., 2005, Introduction to suspended-sediment sampling: U.S. Geological Survey Scientific Investigations Report 2005–5077, CD-ROM.

Perry, C.A., Wolock, D.M., and Artman, J.C., 2004, Estimates of flow duration, mean flow, and peak-discharge frequency values for Kansas stream locations: U.S. Geological Survey Scientific Investigations Report 2004–5033, 651 p.

Rasmussen, P.P., and Ziegler, A.C., 2003, Comparison and continuous estimates of fecal coliform and *Escherichia Coli* bacteria in selected Kansas streams, May 1999 through April 2002: U.S. Geological Survey Water-Resources Investigations Report 03–4056, 80 p.

Rasmussen, P.P., Gray, J.R., Glysson, G.D., and Ziegler, A.C., 2009, Guidelines and procedures for computing time-series suspended-sediment concentrations and loads from in-stream turbidity-sensor and streamflow data: U.S. Geological Survey Techniques and Methods book 3, chap. C4, 53 p.

Rasmussen, T.J., Ziegler, A.C., and Rasmussen, P.P., 2005, Estimation of constituent concentrations, densities, loads, and yields in lower Kansas River, northeast Kansas, using regression models and continuous water-quality monitoring, January 2000 through December 2003: U.S. Geological Survey Scientific Investigations Report 2005–5165, 117 p.

Russell, M.A., Walling, D.E., and Hodgkinson, R.A., 2001, Suspended sediment sources in two small lowland agricultural catchments in the UK: Journal of Hydrology, v. 252, p. 1–24.

Sauer, V.B, and Meyer, R.W., 1992, Determination of error in individual discharge measurements: U.S. Geological Survey Open-File Report 92–144, 21 p.

Shotbolt, L.A., Thomas, A.D., and Hutchinson, S.M., 2005, The use of reservoir sediments as environmental archives of catchment inputs and atmospheric pollution: Progress in Physical Geography, v. 29, p. 337–361.

Simon, Andrew, and Hupp, C.R., 1992, Geomorphic and vegetative recovery processes along modified stream channels of west Tennessee: U.S. Geological Survey Open-File Report 91–502, 142 p.

Simon, Andrew, and Rinaldi, Massimo, 2006, Disturbance, stream incision, and channel evolution—The roles of excess transport capacity and boundary materials in controlling channel response: Geomorphology, v. 79, p. 361–383.

Turnipseed, D.P., and Sauer, V.B., 2010, Discharge measurements at gaging stations: U.S. Geological Survey Techniques and Methods book 3, chap. A8, 87 p.

U.S. Department of Agriculture, Farm Service Agency, 2010, Color aerial photography: Salt Lake City, Utah, U.S. Department of Agriculture, Farm Service Agency, Aerial Photography Field Office, various scales.

U.S. Environmental Protection Agency, 1991, Guidance of water-quality-based decisions—The TMDL process: Washington, D.C., Office of Water, EPA440/4–91–001, 59 p.

U.S. Geological Survey, 2011, National Water Information System (NWISWeb): Information available on the Web, accessed January 26, 2011, at *http://waterdata.usgs.gov/ks/nwis/sw/*.

Vanoni, V.A., ed., 2006, Sedimentation engineering: Reston, Virginia, American Society of Civil Engineers, 418 p.

Wagner, R.J., Boulger, R.W., Jr., Oblinger, C.J., and Smith, B.A., 2006, Guidelines and standard procedures for continuous water-quality monitors—Station operation, record computation, and data reporting: U.S. Geological Survey Techniques and Methods 1–D3, 51 p. plus 8 attachments; accessed November 15, 2008, at *http://pubs.water.usgs.gov/tm1d3*.

Walling, D.E., 2005, Tracing suspended sediment sources in catchments and river systems: Science of the Total Environment, v. 344, p. 159–184.

Waters, T.F., 1995, Sediments in streams—Sources, biological effects and control: Bethesda, Maryland, American Fisheries Society, 251 p.

Williams, G.P, and Wolman, M.G., 1984, Downstream effects of dams on alluvial rivers: U.S. Geological Survey Professional Paper 1286, 83 p.

YSI, 2007, YSI 6136 turbidity sensor: accessed October 4, 2010, at *http://www.ysi.com/media/pdfs/E56-6136-Turbidity-Sensor.pdf*.

Publishing support provided by:
   Rolla Publishing Service Center

For additional information concerning this publication, contact:
   Director, USGS Kansas Water Science Center
   4821 Quail Crest Place
   Lawrence, KS 66049
   (785) 842–9909

Or visit the Kansas Water Science Center Web Site at:
   http://ks.water.usgs.gov

USGS

Juracek—Suspended-Sediment Loads, Sediment Trap Efficiency, and Channel Stability for Kanopolis and Tuttle Creek Lakes, Kansas—SIR 2011–5187

ISBN 978-1-4113-3278-2